Healthcare Supply Chain Management

Healthcare Supply Chain Management

Basic Concepts and Principles

Hokey Min

BUSINESS EXPERT PRESS

First published in 2014 by
Business Expert Press, LLC
222 East 46th Street, New York, NY 10017
www.businessexpertpress.com

ISBN-13: 978-1-60649-894-1 (paperback)
ISBN-13: 978-1-60649-895-8 (e-book)

Business Expert Press Health Care Management Collection

Collection ISSN: 2333-8601 (print)
Collection ISSN: 2333-861X (electronic)

Cover and interior design by Exeter Premedia Services Private Ltd., Chennai, India

First edition: 2014

10 9 8 7 6 5 4 3 2 1

Printed in the United States of America.

In loving memory of my Father,
B.J. Min

Abstract

According to the health data released by the Organization for Economic Cooperation and Development (OECD), the United States spends more per capita on healthcare than any other OECD country. To make it worse, the United States has one of the highest growth rates in healthcare spending. For example, the share of GDP devoted to healthcare spending grew from 9 percent of GDP in 1980 to 16 percent of GDP in 2008. This 7 percent increase in healthcare spending as a share of GDP is one of the largest across the OECD. Currently, U.S. healthcare spending constitutes $2.5 trillion, or 17.3 percent of GDP, with healthcare costs increasing 9 percent annually. To reverse this alarming trend, the Obama administration recently led the effort to dramatically reform healthcare policy, laws, and regulations. One of the most iconic reforms includes the enactment of the Patient Protection and Affordable Care Act on March 23, 2010. Although this act aims to increase the access, fairness, quality, and affordability of health insurance, it is likely to increase the financial burden of some individuals and organizations through higher fees and taxes. That is to say, the success of healthcare reforms often hinges on our ability to find innovative solutions that can allow us to streamline healthcare practices and enhance productivity to the fullest potential. Such solutions that are increasingly put forward by many managerial experts is the adaptation of supply chain principles for healthcare management that are designed to reduce wasteful spending, strengthen connectivity among healthcare partners, and increase visibility of required care and resources.

The main purpose of this book is to provide healthcare policy makers, hospital administrators, pharmaceutical company managers, and other healthcare professionals with practical guidance for leveraging supply chain principles to better manage healthcare resources (e.g., medical equipment, supplies, medicines, nurses, doctors, and capital) and control healthcare costs. This book begins with the introduction of basic supply chain management concepts, terminologies, and tenets. Once the readers grasp the basic principles of supply chain management in a healthcare setting, they will be guided into a number of supply chain strategies that help them make wise day-to-day decisions related to healthcare services. Other included topics are strategic alliances among healthcare partners, value analysis of healthcare services and products, the impact of healthcare reforms on healthcare supply chains, and the development of performance metrics for the healthcare supply chain and benchmarking.

Keywords

healthcare, policy, strategy, supply chain management

Contents

Preface

Since healthcare dictates one's quality of life, it matters more than any other cares or services. Regardless of its importance to public welfare and personal wellbeing, its affordability has been in doubt for a number of years due to rapidly rising costs across the world. Especially, global financial crisis, great recession, and ensuing government budget cuts spurred the national and international debate over the sustainability of affordable healthcare. Since such sustainability lies in the healthcare organization's ability to control costs and improve productivity, the current healthcare practices should be reassessed and fine-tuned with a new way of doing things. As a new way of conducting healthcare practices, this book proposes supply chain principles and expounds how those principles can eliminate the sources of healthcare inefficiency, redundancy, and complacency. Despite the proven benefits of supply chain principles for various managerial practices, relatively few healthcare organizations seem to make it a prioritized solution due in part to a lack of understanding and ignorance of supply chain power. This book is intended to be one of the first that clarifies the basic tenets of supply chain management (SCM) and illustrates how supply chain principles can be leveraged to control healthcare costs and improve long-term productivity. The proper application of supply chain principles to healthcare operations will pave the path toward more affordable and sustainable healthcare services. With this in mind, this book is organized as follows.

Chapter 1 describes the origin of supply chain management, introduces its fundamental conceptual foundation, and describes its benefit potentials for managing healthcare. This chapter also explains a difference between supply chain principles and a traditional way of doing business from a layman's perspective.

Chapter 2 explains how the application of supply chain principles to healthcare operations can transform the healthcare organizations and practices in a positive manner. This chapter also explains what it takes to leverage supply chain concepts to maximize healthcare efficiency.

Chapter 3 describes prerequisites and steps necessary for designing healthcare supply chain frameworks. These steps include the assurance of sustainability, security (or safety), and integrity of healthcare supply chains.

Chapter 4 presents a variety of assessment tools and performance metrics that will help gauge the efficiency and effectiveness of supply chain designs and identify room for continuous improvement of healthcare practices.

Chapter 5, the final chapter, provides the future outlook of healthcare and summarizes emerging trends of healthcare supply chain operations that will shape up future healthcare practices. This chapter also looks at the ways healthcare organizations can innovate their strategic options and managerial practices.

Finally, I would like to thank my colleagues at Business Expert Press who gave me an opportunity to develop an important forum for healthcare supply chain management through the publication of my thoughts and ideas about often overlooked subjects. Also, I would be remiss if I do not appreciate the readers of this book who are patient enough to listen to the quiet voice of the passionate proponent of healthcare supply chain principles.

Hokey Min
Bowling Green, Ohio

CHAPTER 1

Essentials of Healthcare Supply Chain Management

In the United States, human life expectancy jumped from 68.2 years in 1950 to 78.7 years in 2011 (OECD 2013). By 2050, the U.S. life expectancy is expected to reach 88.5 years (Milken Institute 2013). As people live longer, the proportion of aging populations will continue to grow and the need for healthcare services will rise significantly. A growing need for more frequent and better healthcare services can overwhelm the current healthcare system, unless drastic measures can be taken to improve its efficiency and effectiveness. Given chronic shortages of healthcare workers, mounting healthcare operating expenses, and complex government mandates and regulations, we have very limited options to choose from to deal with the current and future healthcare crisis. In this book, we introduce the emerging concept of supply chain management as one of those viable options that can help us not only defuse the healthcare crisis, but also sustain the high level of healthcare productivity.

1.1 What Is Supply Chain Management?

Over the years, many healthcare organizations got engaged in the daily activities of acquiring required medical equipment and supplies, storing essential medicines, distributing medical necessities, and scheduling patient services without coordinating and synchronizing those activities. As these activities are treated as separate organizational functions, we may end up buying medical supplies and pharmacies far more than we need, keeping obsolete medical equipment and archaic technology, and underutilizing healthcare workers. That is to say, the lack of connectivity among these functions can lead to the suboptimization of organizational goals and create inefficiency by duplicating organizational efforts and resources.

To capture the synergy of interfunctional and interorganizational integration and harmonization across the healthcare operations, we need to realize the strategic importance of planning, controlling, and designing a healthcare supply chain as a whole. Generally, a supply chain is referred to as an *integrated system*, which synchronizes a series of interrelated processes in order to: (1) create demand for products; (2) acquire raw materials and parts; (3) transform these raw materials and parts into finished products; (4) add value to these products; (5) distribute and promote these products to either retailers or end-customers; and (6) facilitate information exchange among various interrelated organization entities (e.g., suppliers, manufacturers, distributors, third-party logistics providers, and retailers) (Min and Zhou 2002). Its main objective is to enhance the operational efficiency, profitability, and competitive position of an organization (e.g., hospital) and its supply chain partners (e.g., pharmaceutical manufacturers, healthcare insurers including state healthcare exchanges). More concisely, supply chain management is defined as "the integration of key business processes from end-users through original suppliers that provide products, services, and information and add value for customers and other stakeholders" (Cooper et al. 1997b, 2). A supply chain is characterized by a forward flow of goods and services, a back-and-forth flow of information, and a backward flow of money (or capital) as illustrated by Figure 1.1.

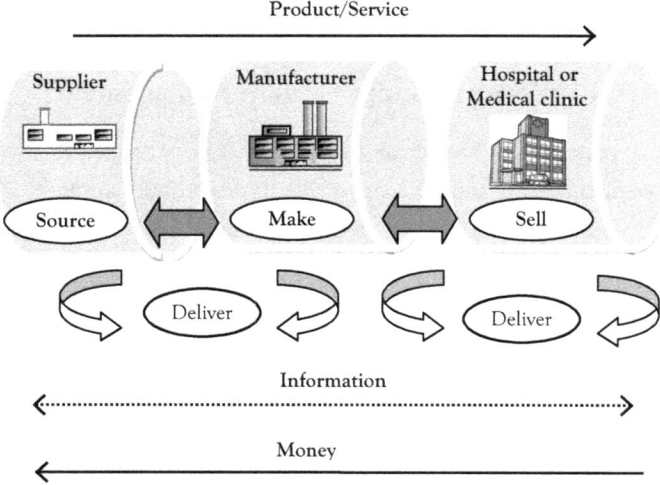

Figure 1.1 Supply chain process

1.1.1 Traditional Versus New Ways of Managing Healthcare

To cope with financial challenges in the midst of economic crisis and budget cuts, many healthcare organizations made conscious efforts to reduce costs by laying-off healthcare workers, postponing investment in equipment and technology modernization, and improving the accuracy of demand forecasts for medical supplies and pharmaceuticals. Although it sounds plausible, this traditional way of saving healthcare costs can backfire because staff reductions through layoffs can exacerbate worker (especially nurse) shortages, the failure to upgrade necessary medical equipment and technology can undermine productivity, and a reliance on forecasts can increase risk and uncertainty associated with the volatile and unpredictable aspects (e.g., emergent care and massive disease outbreaks) of medical supplies and pharmaceuticals. Considering the aforementioned potential pitfalls of traditional cost saving methods, we need to come up with "more innovative and leaner" alternatives. These alternatives should be designed to enhance patient value by eliminating the sources of nonvalue adding activities such as "never events" (e.g., redundant medical procedures, unnecessary surgeries, excessive inventories of medical supplies, and obsolete drugs), administrative red-tapes, and opaque healthcare price mechanism.

One promising alternative that was put forward in the recent past is an adoption of supply chain principles. Put simply, supply chain principles aim to streamline all the healthcare processes related to sourcing needed medical supplies or pharmaceuticals, making healthcare products or creating healthcare services, marketing (selling) healthcare, and delivering healthcare products and services through the elimination of wasteful spending, investment, and activities. The supply chain principle is considered to be a new way of doing business in that it no longer relies heavily on forecasts, it fills the medical order on demand rather than forcing patients to follow the predetermined routine but unnecessary medical procedures, and it empowers patients and healthcare professionals to make appropriate healthcare decisions based on the accurate and timely provision of information throughout the entire healthcare processes.

1.1.2   *Importance of Supply Chain Principles to Healthcare Management*

As discussed earlier, a traditional healthcare management paradigm intends to react to unforeseen patient demand or healthcare service request on a push basis by building buffers such as the Intermediate Care Department for bed-blockers (individuals who occupy the hospital beds because they have no other suitable place to stay for their medical cares), the inventory of medicines (e.g., vaccines) or medical supplies (e.g., syringes) that can mitigate forecasting errors and hides demand planning problems. The traditional paradigm is also characterized by the sequential flow of information from one medical procedure to another. Since the sequential information flow would not give an organization an opportunity to synchronize its functional activities and would impair its visibility throughout the planning processes, the same hidden problems will recur and the vicious cycle of recurring problems will continue without ever addressing them. The best way to break this vicious cycle is to create a proactive system that would allow the organization to see the big picture of the healthcare processes and then analyze the impact of the whole healthcare processes on the organization-wide goals rather than the departmental and functional goals. For example, aggregating demand for the entire healthcare network would allow the Group Purchasing Organization (GPO) to increase its purchasing power or bargaining strength and thus exploit volume discount opportunities for the acquisition of medical supplies and drugs. In addition, centralized purchasing will help the healthcare organization standardize its purchasing practices and avoid duplicated purchases.

As such, to continuously improve healthcare processes, the traditional business paradigm should be replaced by the total system approach that can create a whole greater than the sum of its parts.

Therefore, the total systems approach is considered a major foundation for the supply chain concept. The total systems approach regards the supply chain as an entity that is comprised of interdependent or interrelated subsystems, each with its own provincial goals, but which integrates the activities of each segment so as to optimize the system-wide goals. To elaborate, the total systems approach is referred to as a holistic, integrated approach whereby the entire healthcare processes involving demand planning, purchasing, healthcare service scheduling (e.g., surgery, and nurse and doctor shift scheduling), distribution, and marketing are coordinated to make the best tradeoffs within them so as to achieve the optimal outcome for the whole system. For instance, the decision to create buffers to make healthcare services more readily available to patients will help reduce patient response time and subsequently improve healthcare service quality, but it would incur higher operating costs with a greater chance of extra capacity and idle resources. Without understanding such interdependence of the decision-making processes within the supply chain, the healthcare organization as a whole would continue to suffer from the downward spiral of declining productivity. That is to say, the total systems approach recognizes the fact that the decision made in one of the functions or departments can impact other functions or departments of the organization. As such, the total systems approach that is considered a major conceptual foundation for supply chain principles enables the healthcare organization to assess how changes in healthcare environments affect the healthcare organization's across-the-board total costs and benefits.

1.1.3 Supply Chain Drivers for Healthcare Practices

Despite a high price tag of the healthcare systems in the United States, the United States ranks as one of the worst among the developed countries in terms of healthcare quality. This irony calls for dramatic healthcare reform, which includes the recent enactment of the Patient Protection and Affordable Care Act. Regardless of its intended purposes, healthcare reform is one of the most controversial subjects due to its inherent complexity and dynamics involving multiple stakeholders comprised of patients, their employers (or healthcare buyers and payers), healthcare service providers, insurers, and government entities regulating healthcare services. The moot points regarding healthcare reform often center around the people's right to healthcare, affordability, quality, accessibility, rules and regulations, cost control, and the extent of public financing. Since each stakeholder has a different view of these moot points, it is difficult to establish common goals that would be beneficial to all interested parties. The absence of common goals is likely to obstruct the effort to build partnerships among the interested parties and then share information and resources among them. The inability to share information and resources among the healthcare stakeholders leads to duplicated processes and confusion that have contributed to healthcare inefficiency and ineffectiveness. To develop the common goals, healthcare stakeholders need to figure out what will be the major driving forces (drivers) behind today's healthcare reform involving managerial revolution such as supply chain management. Using the fundamental framework proposed by Min and Zhou (2002), we can classify these drivers into four categories: (1) customer service initiatives, (2) monetary value, (3) information and knowledge transactions, and (4) risk elements.

1.1.3.1   Customer Service Initiatives

Though difficult to quantify, the ultimate goal of healthcare is patient satisfaction. Put simply, patient satisfaction is the degree to which patients are satisfied with the healthcare service received. The following list represents typical service elements in a healthcare supply chain.

- *Service availability*: As an integral part of the healthcare system, healthcare workers play an important role in making healthcare services available to patients when and where those services are needed. Without doctors or nurses, a patient cannot be treated. In spite of their crucial role, there has been a chronic shortage of healthcare workers. According to the World Health Organization (WHO), the world is currently short 7.2 million healthcare workers and will get worse with the expected shortage of 12.9 million healthcare workers by 2035 (Brooks 2013 Thomas et al., 2014). The question remains how disruptive the healthcare supply chain will be without a sufficient number of healthcare workforces and then how adversely healthcare worker shortages influence the quality of healthcare.
- *Response time*: Response time represents an important indicator of the healthcare service quality. Examples of

response time include call-light response time (a speed of answering patient calls), emergency vehicle response time (interval between the time of emergency vehicle request and arrival), patient service time (the expected length of a patient visit), and patient wait time (the length of time interval between when the patient enters the clinic and the time the patient actually leaves the clinic).

1.1.3.2   Monetary Value

The monetary value is generally defined as a ratio of revenue to total cost. A healthcare system can enhance its monetary value through increasing revenue, healthcare coverage, and healthcare worker productivity, while reducing expenditures, service failures, and duplication. More specifically, the monetary value is categorized as follows:

- *Asset utilization*: Asset utilization can be estimated by several different metrics such as net asset turns (a ratio of total gross revenue to working capital), inventory turns (a ratio of annual cost of medical supplies used to average inventory investment), and occupancy rate (the number of inpatient days divided by the number of usable bed days over a specific period such as a year—expressed in percentage).
- *Return-on-investment (ROI)*: This is a typical financial measure determining the true value of an investment. Its measure includes the ratio of net profit to capital that was employed to produce that profit, or the ratio of earnings in direct proportion to an investment.
- *Cost behavior*: In the supply chain framework, cost management requires a broad focus, external to the healthcare organization. Thus, cost may be viewed as a function of strategic choices of the healthcare organization's competitive position, rather than a function of output volume (Shank and Govindarajan 1993). In other words, a traditional cost classification (fixed versus variable cost), which works at the single organization level, may not make sense for the supply chain

network affected by multiple cost drivers (e.g., scope and scale). An alternative cost management principle for a supply chain framework includes activity-based costing (ABC) and cost of healthcare quality.

1.1.3.3   Information and Knowledge Transactions

Information serves as the connection between the various phases of a supply chain, allowing supply chain partners to coordinate their actions and increase visibility (Chopra and Meindl 2004). Therefore, successful supply chain integration depends on the supply chain partners' ability to synchronize and share real-time information. Such information encompasses data, technology, medical know-how, prices, patient lists, patient profiles, patient treatment history, and demand forecasts.

- *Real-time communication*: The establishment of collaborative relationships among supply chain partners is a prerequisite to information sharing. Collaborative relationships cannot be built without mutual trust among supply chain partners and technical platforms (e.g., the Internet, electronic data interchange, extensible markup language, enterprise resource planning, and radio frequency identification) for information transactions. The effectiveness of real-time communication hinges on the supply chain partners' organizational compatibility, which facilitates mutual trust, and technical compatibility, which solidifies electronic links among supply chain partners.
- *Technology transfers*: The collaboration fostered by supply chain partners can be a catalyst for the research and development (R&D) process throughout the supply chain. The rationale being that a healthcare organization, which initiated technology development, can pass its technology or innovative medical know-how to its supply chain partners thereby saving R&D cost and time. Therefore, a successful transfer of technology can help supply chain partners enhance their overall productivity.

1.1.3.4   Risk Elements

The important leverage gained from the supply chain integration is the mitigation of risk. In the supply chain framework, a single supply chain member does not have to stretch beyond its core competency, since it can pool the resources shared with other supply chain partners. On the other hand, a supply chain can pose greater risk of failure due to its inherent complexity and volatility. Braithwaite and Hall (1999) noted that a supply chain would be a veritable hive of risks, unless information is synchronized, time is compressed, and tensions among supply chain members are recognized. Thus, supply chain partners need to profile the potential risks involved in supply chain activities. The following list summarizes such profiles.

- *Risk of healthcare quality failure*: In 2012, more than 100 cases of a rare form of meningitis in nine states in the United States had been traced to tainted batch of steroids manufactured by the New England Compounding Center, Framingham, Massachusetts. As illustrated by the recall of these tainted steroids, the consequences of failing to assure quality at the upstream supply chain can be enormous. This is due to the interdependence of supply chain partners. Similarly, in 2013, Glaxo Smith-Kline (GSK) and Novartis experienced delivery delays of seasonal flu vaccines due to manufacturing delays caused by their suppliers. Such delays created vaccine short-ages for many regions of the United States and wreaked havoc in public healthcare when flu epidemic started. Thus, these kinds of healthcare quality failures should be prevented at the furthest upstream supply chain (if possible, at the initial source of supply).
- *Risk of information failure*: One of the well-known consequences of information failure in the supply chain is a bullwhip effect where production orders of medical supplies or drugs at the upstream supply chain members tend to exaggerate their true demand at the downstream supply chain (e.g., Lee et al. 1997a; Min 2000). Since the bullwhip

effect will create phantom demand and the subsequent overproduction and overstock of unnecessary medical supplies or pharmaceuticals, its risks should be assessed prior to the development of the healthcare supply chain network. One way of reducing such risks is to postpone the final purchasing and shipment of medical supplies or pharmaceuticals until they are needed.

1.1.4   Key Supply Chain Terminology and Concepts

Although supply chain management has been hailed as an innovative way to manage organizational activities or processes in today's decision environments, its concept created a lot of confusion as evidenced by the presence of more than 2,000 different definitions of supply chain management (see Gibson 2005). To avoid confusion and familiarize novice readers with the fundamental concepts of supply chain management, the following key terminologies are introduced and clearly defined.

1.1.4.1   Value

Since the ultimate goal of supply chain management is to serve the customer better by creating or adding value, supply chain management begins with the understanding of customer values and requirements. Generally speaking, "value is the amount customers are willing to pay for what an organization provides them and thus is measured by total revenue, a reflection of the price an organization's product and service commands and the units it can sell" (Porter 1985). Thus, the extent of value created and added by the organization dictates its level of success, because the higher the value, the greater the customer satisfaction and competitive advantages.

1.1.4.2   Push Strategy

A strategy that aims at pushing products or services to the end-user (e.g., patient) through incentives or promotions, this strategy is built on the long-term forecast of anticipated demand as opposed to actual demand from the marketplace. The major downside of this strategy is its inability to meet changing demand patterns and its reactive nature that can create excessive inventory build-ups or inadequate service levels.

1.1.4.3   Pull Strategy

A strategy that uses actual customer demand to determine and schedule the level of service requirements, in this strategy the organization responds to specific customer orders without building buffers. Thus, this strategy can reduce or eliminate the unnecessary waste resulting from excessive capacity or inventory. The major downside of this strategy is its difficulty in creating economies of scale and its requirement for faster response time.

1.1.4.4   Postponement Strategy

A strategy that aims at delaying the downstream portion of some supply chain activities (e.g., assembly and packaging) until customer demand is revealed and the forecasting window shrinks. This strategy is based on the premise that the accuracy of demand forecasting increases with a reduction in the time horizon. The shorter the time window for which the demand is being forecasted, the more accurate demand forecasting will be. One example of the common postponement strategies is to build products in semifinished forms and customize it quickly in manufacturing plants or distribution centers close to customers. This strategy is especially suitable for testing the water for new or innovative products whose potential demand or usefulness is hard to predict.

1.1.4.5   Bullwhip Effect

This phenomenon is generally referred to as an inverse ripple effect of forecasting errors throughout the supply chain that often leads to amplified supply and demand misalignment where orders (perceived demand) to the upstream supply chain member (e.g., the supplier) tend to exaggerate the true patterns of end-customer demand, since each chain member's view of true demand can be blocked by its immediate downstream supply chain member (Lee et al. 1997b; Min 2000). The common symptoms of the bullwhip effect include delayed service deliveries, constant shortages of supplies, frequent customer defection, excessive inventory, erratic service scheduling, and chronic overcapacity problems.

1.1.4.6   Strategic Alliance

The supply chain success is predicated on each supply chain member's willingness to share information with its trade partners. Thus, the establishment of strategic alliance, which increases mutual trust and thus facilitates information sharing among the supply chain members, is crucial for its supply chain success. Strategic alliance is a voluntary relationship formed by multiple independent organizations based on their mutual needs and agreed strategic goals, which nurtures the culture of sharing resources, information, knowledge, and risk among partnering organizations.

1.1.4.7   Core Competency

In a supply chain network where each supply chain member can leverage its partner's resources and information through long-term partnerships, each organization that belongs to the supply chain network should focus on its strength. This strength is considered its core competency. Core competency is referred to as "unique" resources and capabilities such as well-trained workforces (e.g., nurses), efficient facilities (e.g., medical labs), knowhow (e.g., medical expertise and innovative treatments), advanced technology (e.g., radio frequency identification and enterprise resource planning), and customer relations (e.g., patient loyalty).

1.2   Integrating Healthcare Processes through Supply Chain Principles

The term *integration* means a number of different things to different disciplines. Generally, it refers to the organization of different entities or separate units into a harmonious whole. In the healthcare context, the World Health Organization (2008) defined it as "the management and delivery of health services so that clients (patients) receive a continuum of preventive and curative services according to their needs over time and across different levels of the healthcare system." Its ultimate goal is to create value for patients by bringing together different functions and organizations across different parts of healthcare procedures for a single decision, coordinating cross-functional and organizational units through aligned linkages, and then generating economies of scale through the consolidation of multipurpose services (e.g., a series of healthcare service involving pregnancy, childhood birth, and childhood illness care) into a "one-stop shopping" process. Speaking of coordination from the supply chain perspective, there are three dimensions (Ballou et al. 2000): (1) *intrafunctional* coordination that administers the activities and processes *within* the particular function (e.g., coordinated inventory and transportation management within the logistics process) of an organization; (2) *interfunctional* coordination between logistics and purchasing, purchasing and production, and logistics and marketing *among* the functional areas of the organization; and (3) *interorganizational* coordination that takes place *between* legally separated organizations such as pharmaceutical manufacturers and their trading partners (e.g., suppliers). With this in mind, the next subsections will summarize the role of each function and its ties to other related functions in the healthcare supply chain.

1.2.1   Healthcare Supply Chain: Demand Planning

Poirier (1999) argued that the primary objective of supply chain improvements was to serve ultimate customers more effectively and therefore an analysis of the supply chain should focus on the "finish line" (demand), not the "starting point" (supply). To enhance customer values and meet customer requirement, careful planning of demand creation and fulfillment activities is critical to the success of the whole organization. This planning cannot be articulated without understanding the dynamics of interrelated healthcare activities and jointly developing ideas for healthcare process improvement among the intra- and inter-organizational units. In general, demand planning refers to preparations for future demand, which include all the activities associated with the discovery of target markets (customer bases), forecasting of those market trends, analysis of customer behaviors and market dynamics, and fulfillments of customer demand. As such, demand planning is not merely demand forecasting. Although forecasting drives planning, forecasting is the process of predicting future events, whereas planning is the process of selecting the proper courses of actions in response to the forecast (Sanders 2012). The key steps in healthcare demand planning may comprise the following:

1. Collecting and compiling historical healthcare data (including patient data) and then developing patient and service order profiles (e.g., service area demographics, admission patterns, hospital discharge patterns, and census breakdowns by insurance coverage).
2. Making a (statistical) forecast based on the historical data.
3. Developing detailed action plans (e.g., hospital capacity planning, and medical staff planning) for fulfilling anticipated healthcare needs (e.g., outpatient versus inpatient treatment plans, emergency care plans, and financial plans).
4. Prioritizing healthcare services on acute and serious (e.g., life-threatening) healthcare.
5. Communicating healthcare data to healthcare supply chain partners and other stakeholders for predicting future demand.
6. Continually communicating with patients and healthcare supply chain partners and then soliciting feedback from all stakeholders including payors and doctors.
7. Re-examining and updating patient profile and service demand data.

1.2.2 Healthcare Supply Chain: Sourcing

Once the demand plan has been set to fulfill healthcare service order, a healthcare organization should go through a series of interrelated supply chain processes: *sourcing, making, delivering,* and *selling.* At the upstream of the supply chain, sourcing involves acquiring the needed materials and services to meet patient demand. Examples of sourcing activities include: issuance of purchase order, filling purchase requisitions, identification and selection of appropriate suppliers, development and maintenance of long-term supplier relationships, and payments for the purchases. Typical sourcing steps are comprised of the following (see Leenders et al. 2006 for details of purchasing processes):

1. Agreement for the specification of materials or items required by the actual user
2. Recognition of need and priority
3. Description of need and priority
4. Identification of suitable suppliers and then selection of the right source(s) of supply
5. Solicitation of competitive bids or the negotiation of purchasing terms such as pricing and delivery schedules with a number of potential suppliers
6. Evaluation of bids or comparison of offers from the selected suppliers and then determination of right contractual terms based on cost, price, or value analysis
7. Preparation for the purchase order
8. Follow-up and expedition of the order to ensure delivery at the right time
9. Verification (tracing) of the receipt of the order and the invoice of payment
10. Record keeping and update

Sourcing activities are usually triggered by the anticipated demand for healthcare services, or a need for replenishing inventory of medical devices or supplies and pharmaceuticals, or a need for repairing, maintaining, and upgrading medical equipment. Since sourcing decisions significantly affect the healthcare organization's operating costs, a careful sourcing plan has to be developed. One of the common sourcing practices in the healthcare sector is collaborative or group purchasing practices that aim to reduce purchasing costs through volume discounts. Collaborative purchasing (CP) is an arrangement where two or more independent organizations join together—either formally, informally, or through an independent third party—to pool or share their purchasing volume, information, and resources for purchasing goods, services, and technology (Hendrick 1997; Schotanus and Telgen 2007; Gobbi and Hsuan 2010). The purpose of CP is to gain the greater negotiation leverage in contractual terms such as price, quality, and delivery requirements from suppliers than it could be obtained if each organization purchased goods and services alone. CP aggregates and consolidates sourcing activities among peer healthcare organizations in order to streamline purchasing processes for overlapping sourcing needs, exchange information among the participating organizations, and then create synergistic effects in the supply chain. The potential benefits of CP include low purchasing cost, greater access to accurate information, improved asset or capacity utilization, efficient use of scarce human and financial resources in purchasing, increased reliability, and reduced sourcing risk (see Gobbi and Hsuan 2010; Walker et al. 2013). Table 1.1 recapitulates CP's pros and cons in greater detail.

Despite the aforementioned benefits of CP, collaborative (group) purchasing practices are controversial in the healthcare sector. One source of controversies is the "contract administrative fees" (CAF) charged to suppliers (e.g., pharmaceutical manufactures and clinical product manufacturers) by the GPO in the healthcare sector. Although these fees are usually small (less than three percent of the purchase contract price—average of 2.25 percent) and still allow GPOs to reduce

Table 1.1 Pros and cons of collaborative purchasing

Advantages	Disadvantages
• Purchasing cost savings • Better internal exchange of information • Joint learning • Improved negotiation leverage • Less duplicated contract management • More impact on monopolistic supply markets • Improved insight in supply market dynamics • Enhanced ability to attract new suppliers • Pooled purchasing staff and purchasing expertise • Pooled financial resources involved in sourcing • Single channel of communication • Avoidance of potential violations of antitrust laws • Risk sharing among the participating organizations • High degree of mutual trust and professionalism among stakeholders including both buying organizations and suppliers	• High coordination costs • Lack or loss of control over purchasing • Inflexibility • Collaborative governance challenges • Difficulty in building consensus among the participating organization • Difficulties in compliance of unique specifications or quality requirements • Great effort to facilitate standardization of products and services due to organizational incompatibility or varying purchasing needs • Potential free rider problems • Disclosure of sensitive and proprietary confidential information related to sourcing • Declining effect of cost savings • Diminishing opportunities for improvement • Inducement of suppliers' anticompetitive price behavior that can create unfair competition

overall purchasing costs, there are some concerns about CAF's role in reducing the supplier's incentives for product innovation. Also, since GPOs arrange for the referral of business to healthcare suppliers and receive CAF in return for these services, these CAF practices could have triggered the federal antikickback statute. However, the *safe harbor provision* allows GPOs to offer CP opportunities for a healthcare provider (e.g., hospitals, nursing homes, and home health agencies) as long as they meet both of the following rules: (1) The GPO must have a written agreement with each healthcare provider, which provides for either of the two agreements: (a) The supplier from which the hospital or healthcare provider will purchase goods or services will pay a fee to the GPO of 3 percent or less of the purchase price of the goods or services provided by that supplier, and (b) in the event the fee paid to the GPO is not fixed at 3 percent or less of the purchase price of the goods or services, the agreement specifies the exact percentage or amount of the fee. (2) The GPO must disclose in writing to the healthcare provider at least annually, the amount received from each supplier with respect to purchases made by or on behalf of the healthcare provider (Office of the Inspector General 2013). Thanks to the collective bargaining power of the GPOs, the U.S. healthcare industry was reported to save more than $64 billion in 2008 (Goldenberg and King 2009). Considering this past success, CP practices in the healthcare sector will continue to grow in the foreseeable future.

In particular, CP will be most relevant for the purchase of the following goods and services: common-user items such as basic medical supplies (e.g., scissors, forceps, syringes, latex gloves, bandages, and sponges), pharmaceuticals, maintenance–repair–operating (MRO) supplies, security services, janitorial services, diagnostic tools (e.g., stethoscopes and blood pressure monitors), and medical equipment (e.g., wheelchairs, MRI scanners, CT scanners, and X-ray machines). Some notable GPOs in the healthcare sector include: Novation, Amerinet, Premier, MedAsset, The Broadlane Group, HealthTrust Purchasing Group, Consorta, Child Health Corporation of America, along with 14 GPOs belonging to the Healthcare Supply Chain Association (HSCA). Although GPOs are very helpful for saving purchasing costs, it should be noted that it is still up to the healthcare provider to decide which medical products and services are most appropriate in each circumstance and make the most appropriate purchase even after a group purchasing contract is signed.

1.2.3 Healthcare Supply Chain: Making

Sourcing decisions are usually triggered by *making* (production or service creation) decisions. For example, to treat patients, a hospital needs to use syringes and medicines and thus needs to acquire those products from its suppliers. Also, sourcing versus making decisions could be mutually exclusive if those decisions are part of make-buy decisions. For example, the hospital can hire and use its own employees to provide janitorial services, while exercising an option of outsourcing janitorial services from the outside organization. Thus, it is apparent that sourcing and making decisions are related to each other. Considering this important tie between sourcing and making decisions, we must understand how making activities are interacting with sourcing activities in the healthcare sector.

A need for making healthcare products or rendering healthcare services is triggered by patient demand for timely and quality treatments. Also, a patient is often looking for affordable care with the highest possible value (i.e., low price but high quality care). To meet such patient demand, there are three distinctive players in the healthcare supply chain that typically get involved in *making* activities. These are (1) healthcare product manufacturers, (2) pharmaceutical manufacturers, and (3) healthcare service providers (e.g., hospitals, medical clinics, and nursing homes). healthcare product manufacturers (SIC Codes: 2599, 3829, 3842, 3843, 3844, 3851, 8072) are organizations that make a variety of medical equipment, devices, and supplies such as X-ray machines, ultrasound machines, electro-medical equipment, fitness equipment, medical instruments, ophthalmic goods, biotechnology products, and surgical tools. Pharmaceutical manufacturers develop and produce drugs (both generic and brand) licensed for use as medications after they are proven to be safe and potent by the regulatory authority such as the U.S. Food and Drug Administration (FDA). Unlike manufacturers in other industries, the pharmaceutical manufacturer bears a greater risk due to lengthy development, clinical trials, and approval processes. In addition, drugs or pharmaceuticals have become more frequent targets for potential litigations than other products due to their previously unknown side-effects. Furthermore, they are more susceptible to obsolescence than the others due to their limited period of potency. Considering these unique challenges, pharmaceutical production requires a careful planning.

A healthcare provider is an individual (e.g., a doctor of medicine or osteopathy, podiatrist, dentist, chiropractor, clinical psychologist, optometrist, nurse practitioner, nurse-midwife, pharmacist, or a clinical social worker who is authorized to practice by the State and perform within the scope of healthcare practice as defined by the State law) or an institution (e.g., hospital, medical clinic, and nursing home) that provides preventive, curative, specialty, promotional, or rehabilitative healthcare services in a systematic way to individuals, families, or communities (Berkley 2014; MedlinePlus 2014). In particular, given the sizable investment needed for hospital facilities and equipment as well as the high cost of running and administrating hospitals, hospital service planning is one of the most crucial parts of *making* processes in the healthcare supply chain. Its service planning is further compounded by a chronic shortage of qualified healthcare professionals. With little room for margin of error, its planning involves the diagnosis, treatment, and prevention of various kinds of illnesses, injuries, disabilities, and unhealthy habits of a patient. Depending on the location of services, it can be categorized into inpatient, outpatient, and home care service planning. Depending on the level or entry point of the healthcare provision, it can also be classified into primary care (e.g., by family doctors or nurse practitioners), secondary care (e.g., by medical specialists or community hospitals), tertiary care (e.g., by medical centers), and home care (e.g., by rehabilitation aides, occupational therapists, and medical social workers).

Regardless of the types of *making* activities in the healthcare supply chain, one of the most important managerial decisions includes the selection of *make-to-stock* or *make-to-order* strategy. *Make-to-stock* is a proactive approach that uses buffers such as inventory replenishments to meet forecasted demand or anticipated customer order, whereas *make-to-order* is a reactive approach to meet actual demand or a specific customer order on an as-needed basis. The *make-to-stock* strategy relies on more orderly and disciplined plans for making products and managing inventories, while the *make-to-order* strategy intends to responds quickly to abrupt and sudden fluctuations in demand or customer orders without building up unnecessary inventories or creating wasteful buffers (see Table 1.2). Considering the unpredictable and random natures of typical healthcare needs (e.g., emergency cares and responses to infectious disease outbreaks), the *make-to-order* strategy seems to be a better fit for healthcare product manufacturing or healthcare service delivery. However, for preventive care or routine medical checkups or vaccinations, the *make-to-stock* strategy makes sense. As such, a combination of both *make-to-stock* and *make-to-order* has to be considered for maximizing efficiency and effectiveness of the healthcare planning.

Table 1.2 Make-to-stock versus make-to-order strategy

	Make-to-stock	**Make-to-order**
Approach	Proactive	Reactive
Fundamental strategy	Push	Pull
Key principle	Make "enough" well before the orders arrive and then continuously replenish inventory with the anticipation of constant demand	Make only after an order was placed and then make only the exact quantity ordered
Focus	Demand forecast and inventory management	Quick response and customization
Inventory position	Hold inventory at the end of the supply chain	Hold no inventory throughout the supply chain
Production scheduling	Level production	Flexible production
Sourcing plan	Large volume material purchasing	Small volume material purchasing on an as-needed basis
Logistics plan	Consolidation	Just-in-time delivery, frequent shipment with the faster mode of transportation
Example	Production of essential medical supplies such as syringes and gauzes, or production of over-the-counter essential drugs such as aspirins and antibiotics	Production of newly developed medical devices and prescription medicines

Generally speaking, at the downstream of the supply chain (closer to the end-customer or patient) *make-to-order* can be exploited due to a greater need for customized services, while *make-to-stock* can be exploited at the upstream of the supply chain (closer to the supplier) where much of the demand (e.g., chemical ingredients for drugs) is more stable and standardized.

1.2.4 *Healthcare Supply Chain: Selling*

Making decisions are usually triggered by *selling* (marketing or sales promotions) decisions. For example, if there is a high demand for influenza vaccines after seasonal flu outbreaks, a pharmaceutical manufacturer should amp up its production of flu vaccines while a medical device maker should increase its production of syringes that are essential for injecting flu shots for patients. As such, prior to engaging in *making* activities, healthcare organizations and professionals should understand the essence of healthcare sales and its role in the healthcare supply chain. The first step of *selling* healthcare is to understand who healthcare customers (patients) are, what their needs are (or what they value or appreciate most), and how those needs can be met. Without such understanding, it will be difficult for any healthcare service providers to reach out to their customers and offer services that they would really appreciate. Unlike typical retail service environments, customers (patients) cannot choose freely healthcare providers right (most appropriate) for them. The reason is that many patients end up choosing a certain doctor or hospital due to their family doctors' referrals and specific healthcare networks designated by their insurance companies. This makes the healthcare sector less customer-centric and somewhat unruly in terms of pricing. For example, Reinhardt (2006) once discovered that the listed price for chest X-ray examination in one hospital could cost some patients as much as 17 times higher than those of other patients in other hospitals in California. Even at the same hospital, some patients (especially uninsured patients) may get charged far more than others for the same medical treatment or procedure. For instance, in 2004, the rates charged to many uninsured and other self-pay patients for hospital services were often 2.5 times what most health insurers actually paid and more than three times the hospital's Medicare-allowable costs (Anderson 2007). The gaps between rates charged to self-pay patients and those charged to other payers are getting wider than ever before and make it increasingly more difficult for some patients, especially the uninsured, to pay their hospital bills (Melnick and Fonkych 2008). This price discrimination (or differentiated pricing) practice with little transparency in the hospital sector not only creates disservice to patients, but also blurs the actual cost of healthcare services. This complex and opaque pricing practice stems from old business customs in the healthcare sector where hospital charges (prices) are determined by constant negotiations between hospitals and third-party payors such as insurers as well as diverse nomenclatures used by insurance carriers. Since this kind of dynamic pricing may be susceptible to pressures from both managed care and from competing hospitals, the hospital price will be difficult for any patients to predict and thus their choice of a particular hospital or care will become more challenging.

One way to deal with this dilemma is to let the healthcare provider such as the hospital proactively reach out its potential customers (patients) through multiple communication media (including social media) and increase transparency in its pricing practice. In particular, social media may play an important role in facilitating customer-driven healthcare marketing. Though the healthcare sector is slow to adopt social media for its marketing, it offers the healthcare provider less expensive and wide-reaching platforms that can showcase best-in-class healthcare practices (e.g., live broadcast of the surgical procedures, blogging of recent medical reports, and interactive question-and-answer sessions about hospital practices) and then enhance transparency and the subsequent trust with its patients.

1.2.5   Healthcare Supply Chain: Delivering

As we have discussed earlier, the process of *sourcing*, *making*, and *selling* comprises the core of the healthcare supply chain activities. This process, however, cannot be coordinated and then synchronized harmoniously without linking *sourcing*, *making*, and *selling* activities. Such linkage can be made through the *delivering* activity. This *delivering* activity involves the movement, storage, and transfer of goods from the upstream to the downstream part of the supply chain. In a broader sense, it also involves smoothing out the flow of information from upstream to downstream or vice versa. The *delivering* activity that links *sourcing* to *making* will be called inbound logistics, while the *delivering* activity linking *making* to *selling* will be dubbed outbound logistics. Although the *delivering* activity is often misconstrued as a mere supporting function, it is considered a primary value-adding or value-creating function in the supply chain. Especially with rising fuel cost and growing time-sensitivity of delivery requirement, the *delivering* activity can have a profound impact on the overall efficiency of the supply chain and the organization's bottom line. For example, it was estimated that up to 46 percent of a hospital's operating budget was spent on logistics-related activities (Landry and Phillipe 2004). This disproportionally high percentage of logistics costs in the healthcare sector may be due to its inherent nature of business that frequently uses obsolescence-prone drugs and medical supplies, necessitates emergency care requiring the premium (expensive) mode of transportation, and relies on the multiple-layers of complex distribution and marketing channels.

Therefore, logistics (*delivering* activity) deserves more attention from healthcare professionals and needs to be re-engineered to reduce or eliminate the sources of waste. One of those logistics re-engineering efforts includes: *point-of-use distribution* that allows major distributors to replenish all the inventories of essential medical supplies and drugs for the hospital and then deliver them directly to the point of use (Landry and Phillipe 2004). Thus, this practice eliminates the need for holding and managing inventory at the hospital stockroom and thus helps the hospital save costs. Another example includes the adoption of emerging information and communication technology (ICT) such as radio frequency identification (RFID) tools that aimed to increase inventory visibility and accuracy by better tracing inventory location and movement (Carr et al. 2010). Also, to better utilize storage space for medical supplies while conserving start-up investment funds for additional permanent facilities, the hospital may consider introducing the modular storage area where a number of different medical supplies can be stored at one location and handled on a temporary basis for multipurpose medical treatments and emergency responses.

1.2.6   Interfaces among Healthcare Functions

In earlier sections, we discussed about the need for coordination across different functions of the supply chain to avoid the suboptimization of organizational goals. To better coordinate a series of *sourcing, making, selling,* and *delivering* activities in the healthcare supply chain, we should understand the interdynamics among them and then create dialogue channels among them to facilitate interfaces among them through constant communication and information sharing. For instance, *making* medical equipment such as the X-ray machine requires acquisition of its parts such as tubes, operating consoles, and film holders, which triggers a set of *sourcing* activities. In turn, the quality of these purchased parts often determines the quality of an X-ray machine as a finished good, which is intended for *selling* and then *delivering* to a customer (e.g., hospital). Thus, *sourcing* (purchasing) is tied to *making* (production), *selling* (marketing), and *delivering* (logistics).

To elaborate, an effort to lower logistics costs by consolidating smaller shipments into a larger shipment and using the slower mode of transportation would increase customer response time and thus hurt customer services due to delayed deliveries. On the other hand, quick response or just-in-time (JIT) delivery will improve customer services by delivering products at the right time, while it may increase transportation cost through the nonstop delivery or the use of a faster (premium) mode of transportation. That is to say, logistics directly influences the customer service part of marketing. As graphically displayed in Figure 1.2, logistics contributes to the place dimension of the marketing mix by creating both spatial (e.g., moving medical devices to the hospital) and temporal (e.g., holding essential drugs until the patient demands it) utilities for the customer. In the meantime, sales promotion through heavy advertisement or discounted pricing will encourage the customer to order or buy the marketed product. Once the product is ordered and purchased, its real-time point-of-sales (POS) information fed by the retailer (e.g., pharmacies and supermarkets) would prepare for the manufacturer (e.g., pharmaceutical maker) to produce ordered goods and then fulfill the customer order using inventories kept in its warehouse or distribution center. To produce goods that the customer ordered, the

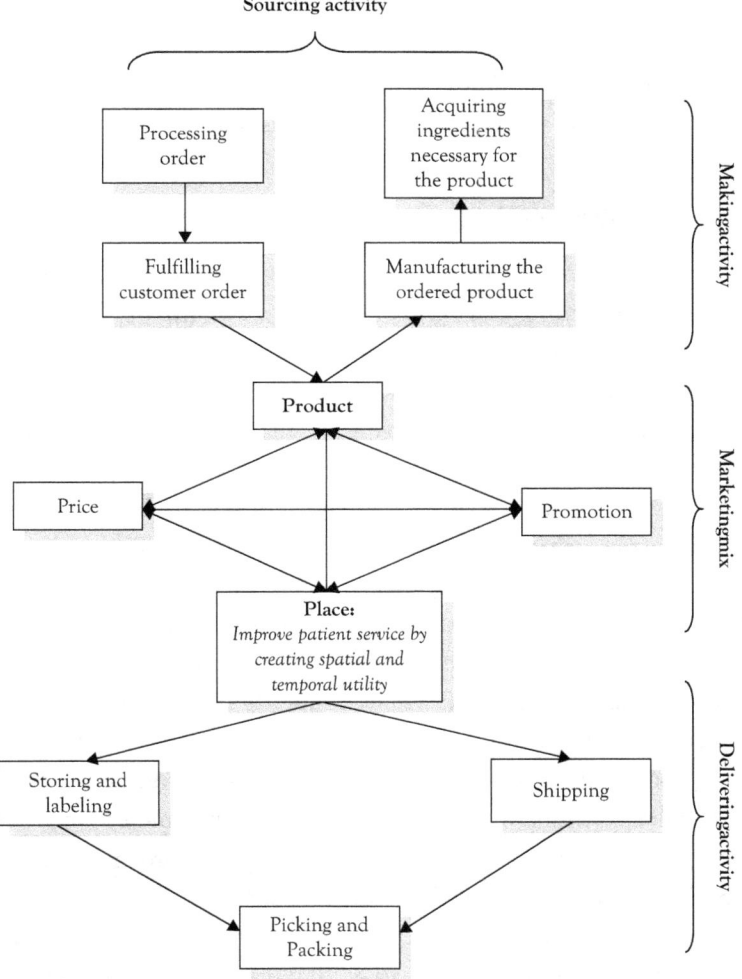

Figure 1.2 Interfaces among different functions

manufacturer needs to acquire the necessary raw materials, parts, and components from its sources of supply. In other words, a production activity (e.g., manufacturing medical devices ordered by the hospital) will trigger sourcing activities such as the acquisition of necessary ingredients while sourcing activities such as order processing and fulfillment will trigger a production activity. This example illustrates the influence of marketing on production, logistics, and purchasing. Considering these interdependences among purchasing, production, logistics, and marketing, the balancing acts are needed to achieve the desired benefits of the healthcare organization as a whole. Such balancing acts can be put together effectively through supply chain integration.

1.2.7   *Developing Healthcare Supply Chain Maps*

Since supply chain coordination goes far beyond the integration of *sourcing*, *making*, *selling*, and *delivering* processes within the organization, we need to conceptualize how these processes are linked to each other through the involvement of multiple external partners. For example, to constantly replenish daily healthcare necessities such as syringes, the hospital should purchase those items from syringe manufacturers. To meet the hospital demand for syringes and sustain their production capability, these manufacturers, in turn, need to acquire key materials such as plastics comprising syringes from their own suppliers (e.g., plastic makers). These plastic makers/suppliers also need to acquire the plastic's key ingredients such as hydrocarbon originated from oil from its own suppliers. As such, if there is a shortage of oil, it will eventually impact the availability and subsequent price of syringes. An increase in syringe price will, in turn, increase the expenses of treating patients at the hospital. Considering this interdependence and connection among the supplier's suppliers and their next-tier suppliers through a complex web of relationships (or links), it would be beneficial for us to visualize such relationships. One way of doing so is the development of a supply chain map. A supply chain map is a graphical form of a communication device that helps supply chain policy and decision makers visualize key information regarding distribution channel dynamics, strategic business environments, communication flows, physical product flows, relationships among supply chain partners, and geographical representations of supply chain infrastructure and partners (Gardner and Cooper 2003). This map is helpful for having a clear picture of how all the supply chain partners are linked and connected, where the potential sources of supply chain disruptions or vulnerabilities and risks are, and who may be the right supply chain partners. This map can be drawn vertically or horizontally as illustrated by Figure 1.3a and 1.3b.

Upstream

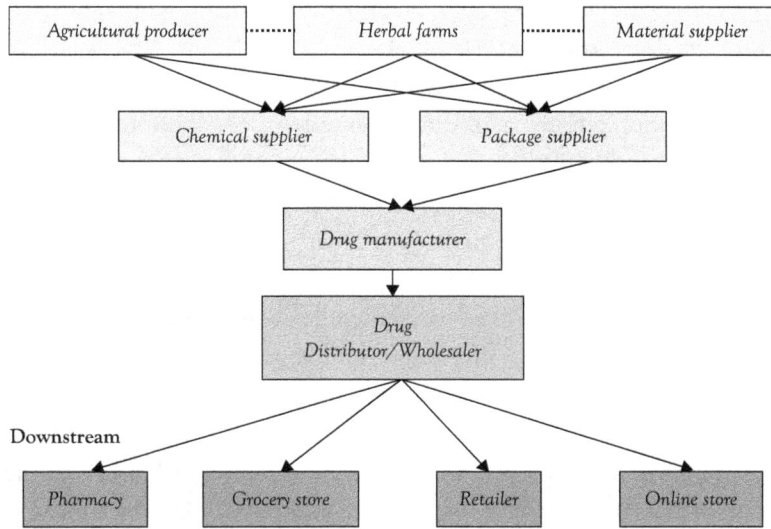

Figure 1.3a *Example of a vertical supply chain map for over-the-counter drugs*

In a vertical SC map, a supply chain flow can be displayed from top to bottom. Usually, the top of the map shows the upstream supply chain activity (e.g., sourcing) while the bottom portion of the map shows the downstream supply chain activity (e.g., distribution and sales). For example, in its simplistic form, the over-the-counter drug (e.g., aspirin) can be sold at brick-and-mortar outlets such as the local pharmacy (e.g., Walgreen), grocery store (e.g., Kroger), and chain store (e.g., Walmart), while it can be purchased online (e.g., drugstore .com). This drug is usually provided by a drug distributor such as Cardinal Health and a wholesaler such as A.F. Houser. These middlemen obtain the drug from its manufacturer such as Johnson & Johnson, Pfizer, Roche, GlaxoSmithKline, and Eli Lilly. These pharmaceutical manufacturers need chemical ingredients of the drug and a plastic bottle that can contain the finished drug. These ingredients (e.g., acetylsalicylic acid) will be acquired by first-tier suppliers such as chemical suppliers and package suppliers (e.g., Drug Plastics and Glass Co.). These first-tier suppliers need to acquire their raw materials and virgin ingredients from second-tier suppliers such as agricultural producers, herbal farms (e.g., ginseng farms), and material suppliers (e.g., petrochemical producers for the drug bottle maker).

Since the supply chain activity encompasses service flows, the horizontal supply chain map can graphically display healthcare service processes. For example, Figure 1.3b graphically depicts which healthcare providers are involved in patient care. To elaborate, if a patient gets sick, he or she will first consult with his or her primary care physician (e.g., family doctor) for the initial diagnosis or medical advice and then he or she will be sent to either the local medical clinic or the secondary physician (e.g., specialist) for further diagnosis. The secondary care physician often sends the patient to medical labs for further tests before deciding on any necessary medical treatment. If the in-patient care (e.g., surgery), urgent care, or more thorough test is needed, the patient will be sent to the general hospital for further diagnosis or treatment. Once treatment is provided, medical bills will be sent to the patient's insurance company for payment or reimbursement.

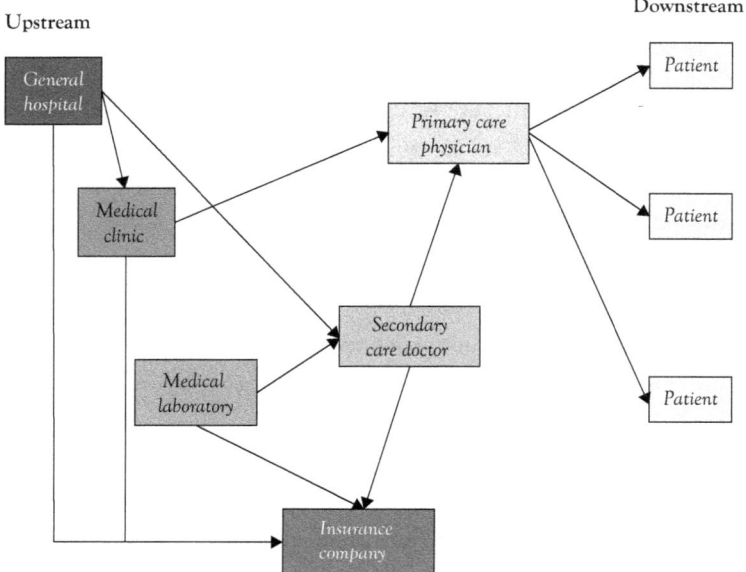

Figure 1.3b Example of a horizontal supply chain map for patient care

1.3   Supply Chain Management as a Catalyst for Value-Adding Healthcare Processes

The provision of healthcare involves many players: (1) *payor* (e.g., government, employer, and individual); (2) *healthcare service provider* (e.g., doctors, hospitals, pharmacies, and integrated delivery network); (3) *healthcare product maker* (e.g., drug manufacturers, medical device and equipment makers); (4) *insurers* (e.g., healthcare exchanges, health maintenance organization, and preferred provider organization); (5) *channel intermediaries* (e.g., distributors, wholesalers, and GPO). The presence of these many players in the healthcare sector means a high likelihood of conflicts, miscommunication, overlap, and fragmentation that can create inefficiencies and thus offer low customer value (i.e., low quality but expensive healthcare services). To avoid these inefficiencies, we have to embrace the idea of supply chain management, which can help us break the hidden silos among different healthcare players and then harmonize their conflicting interests. The adoption of supply chain principles starts with the identification of main sources of troubles that undermine healthcare efficiency. The next subsections will discuss about ways to uncover the root causes of healthcare inefficiency and then develop action plans to improve healthcare efficiency throughout the entire healthcare processes.

1.3.1   Sources of Healthcare Waste

As discussed earlier, the healthcare sector is notorious for its widely varying pricing and quality structures. Unlike other sectors, it is not unusual to see substantial differences in cost and quality for the same type of care across healthcare service providers, geographical areas, and service recipients (i.e., patients). This unique but unfair practice may have made many healthcare service providers insensitive to their ability to provide customer value because such a practice is considered to be business norm or business as usual. In other words, this kind of practice gives the healthcare service provider little incentive to improve their operations. The common acceptance of this kind of practice by the healthcare sector may originate from the fact that the end-user (patient) of healthcare services is not necessarily a payor and thus the end-user does not necessarily care about the entire expense (bill), but his or her portion of copayment or deductible amount.

Since the cost of switching to other alternative service providers is not that high for the patient, he or she tends to tolerate unfair pricing. To make matters worse, the patient usually has no or little access to alternative pricing information in the healthcare marketplace and thus his or her comparison shopping opportunity is limited. The aforementioned problem with a lack of comparison shopping is further compounded by the limits and constraints imposed by healthcare insurers. While a lack of motivation for value creation on the part of a healthcare service provider is an ongoing concern, the fragmented structure of the healthcare sector is another serious concern.

As Burns et al. (2002) pinpointed, fragmentation complicated the task of connecting the multiple players at each stage of healthcare processes and posed difficulty in standardizing the healthcare practices throughout the processes. For example, patient care is often structured around the specialties of physicians and thus the patient receives discrete service from each physician with separate procedures and billing. This discrete service can be a source of inconsistency and duplications that cause inefficiency. As a matter of fact, it was reported that 30 percent of the $2.3 trillion spent on healthcare was wasted due to business-as-usual attitudes in the healthcare sector (NEHI 2014). To elaborate, specific examples of sources of this waste include the following (Delaune and Everett 2008):

- Variation in the intensity of clinical and surgical care across the hospital and geographical region (e.g., varying frequencies of coronary artery bypass surgeries)
- Misuses of drugs and medications
- Lack of compliance with clinical guidelines (e.g., overuse of antibiotics), raising concerns about the physician's decision-making procedure
- Underuse of cost-effective diagnostic tests
- Overuse of nonurgent emergency department (ED) care
- Limited adoption of ICT in areas such as medical decision support and care coordination

In an effort to prevent the recurrence of this waste, we introduce the emerging management techniques that can help the healthcare service provider identify the sources of waste systematically in the following subsections.

1.3.2 Identifying Nonvalue Adding Healthcare Processes Using Value Stream Mapping

As discussed in the previous section, any processes that only consume resources but do not add value to the healthcare product or service will be considered waste. This waste can take a variety of forms: *service delays* that will make patients wait for a long time; *quality failures* resulting from the use of substandard and counterfeit drugs, defective medical equipment, and erroneous diagnosis; *redundancy* that requires repeated medical procedures and lab tests; *obsolescence* emanating from the unused or expired inventory (e.g., expired drugs); *miscommunication* that leads to poor medical decisions by impairing transparency and visibility; *interrupted movement* caused by poorly designed logistics flows (e.g., lengthy delivery routes) or poor motion studies (e.g., hospital layout requiring additional motion for surgery or patient transfer); and *underutilized talent* as a result of role conflicts or misassignment of healthcare workers. One effective way to identify and eliminate this kind of waste is to conduct value analysis that is designed to create maximum value in meeting customer (patient) demand. In a broad sense, value analysis is disciplined thinking that studies the function of a material, part, component, or system in an organized and systematic fashion to identify unnecessary costs (Miles 1972; Fowler 1990). Put simply, it is a better way to get the job done to provide the customer with what he or she wants for a lesser cost. One of the important purposes of value analysis is to provide a decision maker with an early warning signal for prompt corrective actions before it is too late. Such a signal can be visually displayed through value stream mapping. As a blueprint for lean transformation, value stream mapping is a graphical tool that gives a decision maker (e.g., hospital administrator) a broad picture of the entire healthcare processes, both value and nonvalue adding activities, and all product, service, and information flows to identify where to focus for resource allocation (Hines and Rich 1997; Rother and Shook 2003; Lasa et al. 2008). It is comprised of the following three major steps (Rother and Shook 2003):

1. Document Current State Value Streams
   - Thoroughly understand current conditions and identify the cause of waste

- Analyze what it looks like now to figure out what to change
- *Make Non-Value Added (WASTE) Visible*
2. Document Future State Value Streams
   - Draw the lean plan in the future through brainstorming
   - Describe what the future processes look like to determine what improvement should be made
   - *Eliminate or Reduce Non-Value Added (WASTE)*
3. Document Implementation
   - Develop action plans, task journey from the current state to the future state, and then track progress
   - *Implement and Document Processes with less WASTE*

Examples of value stream mapping application to healthcare include (Lummus et al. 2006; King et al. 2006; Jimmerson 2009; Teichgräber and de Bucourt 2012): elimination of bottlenecks in the medical clinic's patient recovery room, reduction in turnaround time for pathologist reports from an anatomical pathology lab, procurements of endovascular stents, and the improvement of patient flows in EDs.

Figure 1.4 illustrates the example of value stream mapping for patient surgery procedures. This value stream map shows redundancy (e.g., repeated medical history checks) and a long patient waiting time that was compounded by a lengthy process of locating bed. Also, a transition from one to another succeeding process seems to be too long and consequently increases the level of distress for the patient. The potential sources of problems causing a long wait include the following instances:

- The patient's health record or history was manually checked.
- Bed board data are inaccurate and not up to date and thus bed assignment is delayed.
- A hospital administrative staff is not aware of which room's bed requires clean-up.
- A patient is forced to wait even after the room or bed is available because a sufficient number of nurses are not on duty on the floor and out-of-hospital doctors are not ready to treat the patient immediately.
- Unorganized nurse shift scheduling creates a schedule conflict with nurses' break time and changeover.

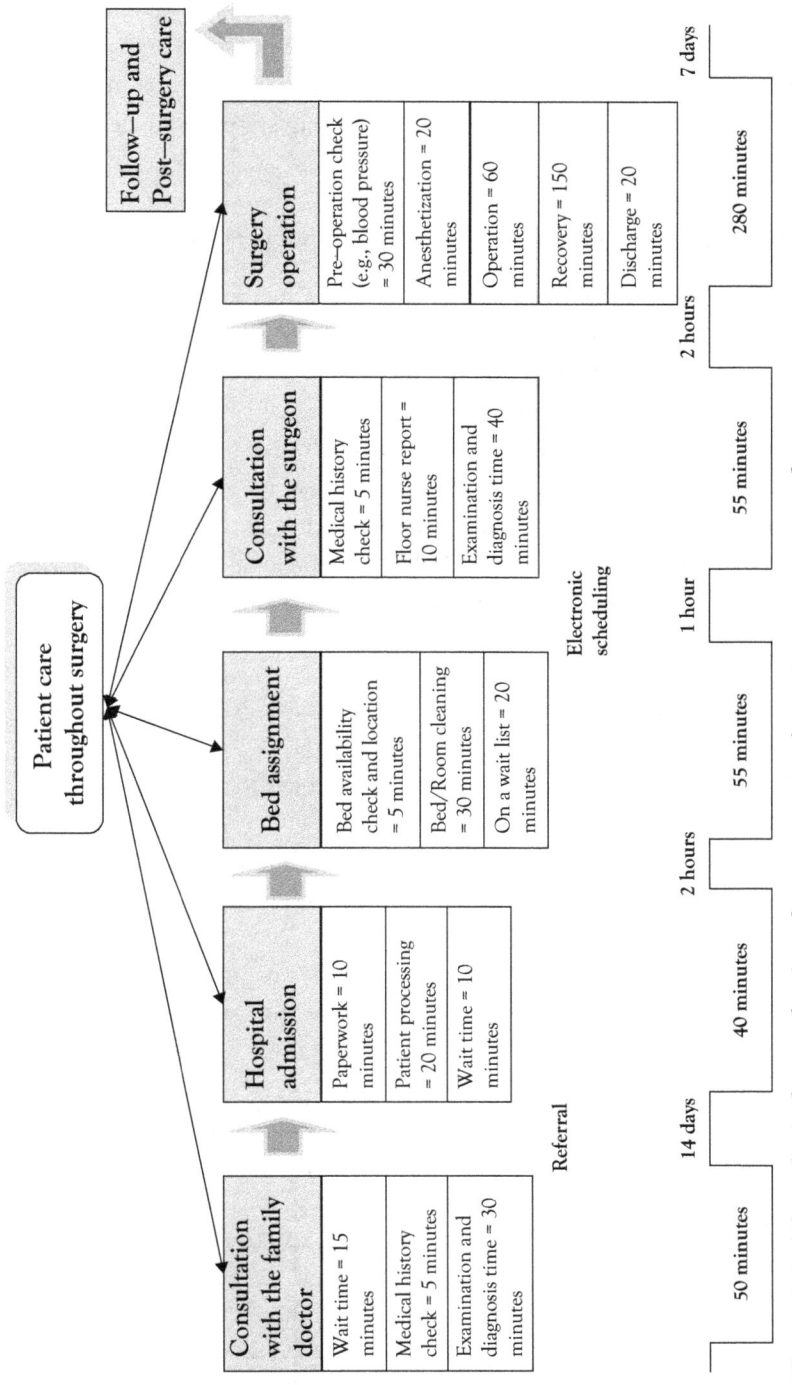

Figure 1.4 A hypothetical example of a value stream map for patient surgery procedures

As illustrated in this example, the value stream map helps identify the main sources of problems with a visual aid and then provides a roadmap for process improvements (e.g., online check and tracking for room or bed availability, an automated nurse shift scheduling system, and electronic health record transfers).

1.3.3 Six Sigma for the Lean Healthcare Supply Chain

Six Sigma is a lean thinking process that was pioneered by Bill Smith at Motorola in 1986. It was originally defined as a metric for measuring defects and improving quality, and a methodology to reduce defect levels below 3.4 defects per one million opportunities (DPMO) as summarized in Table 1.3 (Pyzdek and Keller 2003). Driven by the deep understanding of customer needs and desires, *Six Sigma* seeks to find and eliminate the causes of defects and variability by focusing on value-creating or value-adding processes that are critical to customers and bringing financial returns to the organization. The main goals of *Six Sigma* are as follows (Averboukh 2006):

1. Improve the efficiency of value-adding activities within healthcare processes
2. Sustain process changes, particularly through data-based business process control
3. Reduce loss of time, effort, and money due to defects and failures in specific process steps and subsequent nonvalue-adding activities

As stated in these goals, the concept of *Six Sigma* is complementary to that of value analysis in that both intend to eliminate nonvalue-adding waste.

Table 1.3 Sigma quality level and its corresponding yield

Sigma	Corresponding yield	DPMO
1	30.9 %	690,000
2	69.2%	308,000
3	93.3%	66,800
4	99.4%	6,210
5	99.98%	320
6	99.9997%	3.4

Thus, *Six Sigma* can be incorporated into the value analysis framework. Within that framework, *Six Sigma* is comprised of five phases as shown in Figure 1.5 (Chowdhury 2001; Harry and Schroeder 2006):

1. **Define** the process improvement goals that are consistent with customer (patient) demands and organizational achievement thresholds. This process includes defining the outline of the efforts and the leadership of the improvement project.
2. **Measure** the current process after mapping it out and then collect relevant data for future comparison and evaluation. This process also looks for clues for the root causes of the current problems.

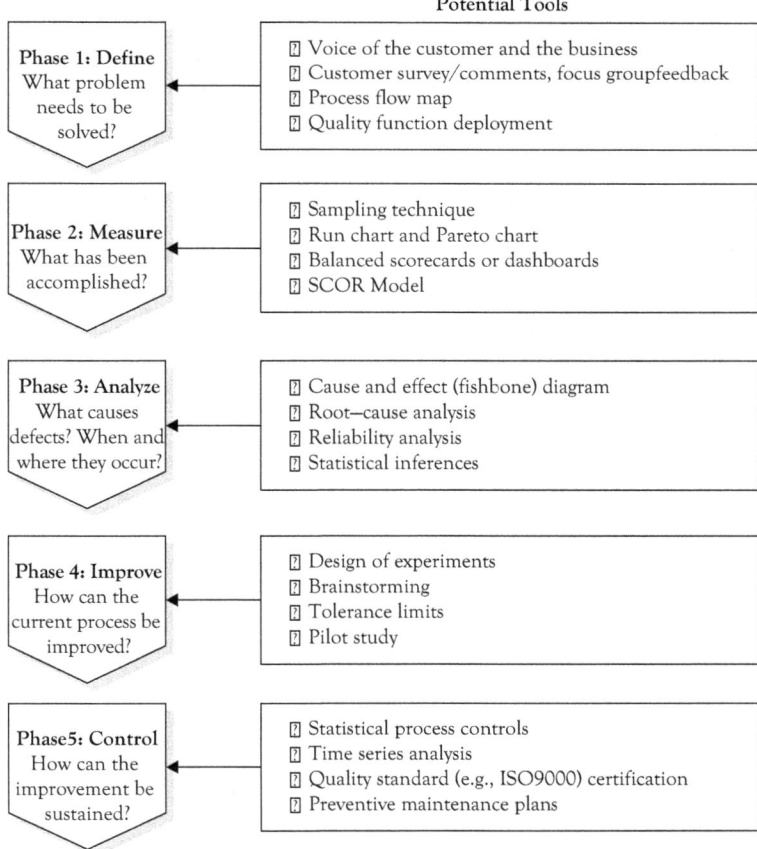

Potential Tools

Phase 1: Define
What problem needs to be solved?

- ⬚ Voice of the customer and the business
- ⬚ Customer survey/comments, focus groupfeedback
- ⬚ Process flow map
- ⬚ Quality function deployment

Phase 2: Measure
What has been accomplished?

- ⬚ Sampling technique
- ⬚ Run chart and Pareto chart
- ⬚ Balanced scorecards or dashboards
- ⬚ SCOR Model

Phase 3: Analyze
What causes defects? When and where they occur?

- ⬚ Cause and effect (fishbone) diagram
- ⬚ Root–cause analysis
- ⬚ Reliability analysis
- ⬚ Statistical inferences

Phase 4: Improve
How can the current process be improved?

- ⬚ Design of experiments
- ⬚ Brainstorming
- ⬚ Tolerance limits
- ⬚ Pilot study

Phase5: Control
How can the improvement be sustained?

- ⬚ Statistical process controls
- ⬚ Time series analysis
- ⬚ Quality standard (e.g., ISO9000) certification
- ⬚ Preventive maintenance plans

Figure 1.5 Five phases of Six Sigma

Source: Adapted and significantly modified from Goldsby and Martichenko (2005).

3. **Analyze** to diagnose and verify relationship and causality of factors through cause-and-effect diagrams. Determine what the relationship is and attempt to ensure that all factors have been considered. This process also may involve value stream mapping.

4. **Improve** or optimize the process based on the statistical technique such as the design of experiments and then verify the effectiveness and efficiency of the newly changed process. This process often involves brainstorming.

5. **Control** to ensure that any variances are corrected before they result in defects based on control charts. Set up pilot runs to establish process capability, transition to production, and thereafter continuously measure the process and institute control mechanisms.

Ranges of healthcare problems that were successfully tackled by *Six Sigma* include (de Koning et al. 2006): shortening the length of stay in chronic obstructive pulmonary disease patients; reducing errors in invoices received from temporary agencies; revising the terms of payment; allowing parents to room in with their sick children; reducing the number of patients requiring intravenous antibiotics; and shortening the preparation time of intravenous medication. Despite promising application potentials of *Six Sigma* for healthcare, *Six Sigma* is not a panacea because it is often complex and only effective at fixing the narrow scope of the existing process instead of aiding the healthcare organization in developing innovative ideas or processes.

CHAPTER 2

Supply Chain Transformation in the Healthcare Sector

In 2011, the world's total healthcare spending including preventive and curative healthcare, family planning, nutrition support, and emergency aids accounted for 10.1 percent of the world gross domestic product (GDP) (World Bank 2013). Despite a recent slowdown of the spending growth, healthcare expenditures are expected to escalate for years to come. For instance, in 2011 healthcare expenditures rose to 9.4 percent of GDP on average across the 34 OECD countries, from 5.5 percent in the second half of the last decade (2006 to 2010) (OECD 2013). As of 2011, total healthcare spending in the United States was 17.7 percent of GDP, and if unchecked it is expected to account for 26 percent of GDP by as early as 2035 (Congressional Budget Office 2011; OECD 2013). In some developing countries, it will rise even faster. In China, healthcare spending is expected to rise to 6.4 percent of its GDP by 2060 from 1.9 percent in the second half of the 2000s (de la Maisonneuve and Martins 2013). To reverse this alarming trend, both public and private sectors have focused their attention to the effectiveness and efficiency of healthcare services. Examples of sources of healthcare waste undermining healthcare effectiveness and efficiency include erroneous diagnosis, malpractice litigation, unnecessary and redundant tests, insurance fraud, treating preventable infections and injuries, excessive administrative costs, high drug and medical device inventory costs, and improper payments (e.g., abusive billings and kickbacks). For instance, Goldman (2012) reported that healthcare fraud and abuse alone added as much as $98 billion to U.S. Medicare and Medicaid spending in 2011. In addition, as summarized in Table 2.1, Mckinsey & Company found that days

Table 2.1 Comparative inventory metrics

	Days of inventory	Obsolescence (% of sales)	Manufacturing lead time (in days)
Pharmaceuticals	258 days	3.1%	120–180 days
Medical devices	153	2.8	120–180
Fast-moving consumer goods	72	0.5	3–7

Source: Ebel et. al. (2013).

of inventory for both pharmaceuticals and medical devices were two to four times longer than those of the typical fast-moving consumer goods, while its level of obsolescence was six times higher than that of their consumer good counterparts (Ebel et al. 2013). Thus, it is not surprising that inventory costs associated with drugs and medical devices are unusually high. These illustrated symptoms are telltale signs of fragmented, disjointed, and uncoordinated supply chain activities in the healthcare sector. Considering an urgent need for better supply chain management for healthcare services, the following sections will discuss ways to transform the traditional healthcare processes into more innovative processes embracing supply chain principles.

2.1   External Factors that Reshape the Healthcare Practices

The world is experiencing demographic shifts as people live longer. For example, in 2010, more than 58 million U.S. adults were in their 50s and early 60s—approximately 19 percent of the population (Smolka et al. 2012). The aging of world population requires new thinking about healthcare services for this rapidly growing population sector. As the baby boomer generations enter their silver years, they are more prone to suffer from a various type of illness and disability. As a matter of fact, from 2000 to 2012, the number of individuals filing for disability benefits increased over 60 percent (Social Security Administration 2013). An increase in the number of individuals with debilitating diseases such as Alzheimer's and Parkinson's diseases, coupled with a lack of geriatric cares or long-term care facilities for the elderly, poses many new healthcare challenges. Additionally, the recent healthcare reform such as the Patient Protection and Affordable Care Act dramatically changes healthcare practices. Furthermore, recent increases in natural disasters such as Hurricane Sandy and Irene have created another healthcare challenge associated with emergency preparedness and public health concerns. Other overlooked healthcare trends that may impact healthcare practices include changes in life-style and social fabrics that lead to a rapid rise in the number of individuals suffering from substance abuses and mental and psychiatric disorders. In the following subsections, we will discuss how aforementioned exogenous factors (e.g., demographic shifts, healthcare reforms, disaster risks, and sociological trends) can reshape healthcare practices.

2.1.1   Implications of the Affordable Care Act for Healthcare Supply Chains

Perhaps the Patient Protection and Affordable Care Act (ACA) is the most radical legislative transformation of the U.S. healthcare system in the last few decades, because it fundamentally changes every aspect of healthcare. The core elements of the ACA are: (1) a mandate for individuals and businesses requiring an approved level of health insurance (e.g., a ban on exclusion of children younger than 19 years of age with preexisting conditions, and coverage of clinical preventive benefits); (2) a complete or partial payment for the required health insurance through federal subsidies (e.g., health exchanges and Medicaid, and government as an insurer for the elderly and the poor); (3) extensive new requirements on the health insurance industry (e.g., public justification of rate hikes by the insurance company); and (4) numerous regulations on healthcare practices (e.g., hospital readmission) (Huntington et al. 2011; U.S. Department of Health and Human Services 2012). Basically, the ACA establishes the basic legal protections that guarantee near universal access to affordable health insurance coverage, from cradle to grave. When fully implemented, the Act will cut the number of uninsured Americans by more than half. The law will result in health insurance coverage for about 94 percent of the U.S. population, reducing the uninsured by 31 million people, and increasing

Medicaid enrollment by 15 million beneficiaries. Still, approximately 24 million people are expected to remain without coverage (Congressional Budget Office 2010). The primary purposes of the ACA are: (1) to achieve near-universal coverage and to do so through shared responsibility among governments, individuals, and employers; (2) to improve the fairness, quality, and affordability of health insurance coverage; (3) to improve healthcare value, quality, and efficiency while reducing wasteful spending and making the healthcare system more accountable to a diverse patient population; (4) to strengthen primary healthcare access while bringing about longer-term changes in the availability of primary and preventive healthcare; (5) to make strategic investments in the public's health, through both an expansion of clinical preventive care and community investments (Rosenbaum 2011). Despite these optimistic goals, its impact on the positive outcomes is still unknown or ambiguous at best. Though the true impact of the ACA will not be fully realized for years to come, it is expected to influence the preventive care (including early detection of diseases), primary care, healthcare delivery, payment system, reimbursement structure, healthcare quality measures, and reporting mechanism. That is to say, from a supply chain standpoint, the ACA is likely to dramatically alter the patient and information flows not to mention interrelationship among healthcare stakeholders (e.g., a relationship between healthcare providers and insurers, and a relationship between governments and insurers).

2.1.2   Implications of Graying Population for Healthcare Supply Chains

More than 20 percent of the estimated U.S. population will be over the age of 65 by 2030. This age group represents the fastest growing cohort within the U.S. population. Currently, approximately 47 million people are over the age of 65 in the United States; by 2050 they will number more than 83 million (U.S. Census Bureau 2013). Similarly, by 2060 the percentage of people aged over 65 will be about 29.5 percent in the Europe Union (EU) 27 countries (European Commission 2014). The aging of the population across the world presents vast healthcare challenges due to the elderly's higher vulnerability to diseases and their gradual decline in physical and mental capacity. To meet these challenges, we must reinvent and restructure our healthcare system in such a way that it can support the unique needs of the elderly people for living healthy, independently, and productively. Generally speaking, aging is accompanied by declines in visual and auditory acuity, a slow reaction and response time, dwindling motor skills and agility, and deteriorating cognitive abilities such as lapses in memory and attention (Czaja and Sharit 2009). These age-related healthcare issues necessitate more *long-term* (e.g., cares for the chronically ill and disabled patients), *transitional* (e.g., cares during transfer from a hospital to a nursing home), and *home* cares (e.g., around-the-clock in-home cares and assisted living) as well as new medical devices such as beepers and electronic pill dispensers that can remind older people about medication schedules. Also, many of the elderly retirees who live on a fixed income cannot afford to cover out-of-pocket expenses, thereby requiring more government aids for financing healthcare services. Coping with unique and complex healthcare challenges illustrated earlier, healthcare providers should design the uninterrupted, sustainable healthcare supply chain that can integrate daily living assistances (e.g., bathing, cooking, dressing, housekeeping, and transportation) with medical treatments (e.g., medications and rehabilitations).

2.2   Change Management for Leveraging Healthcare Supply Chains

A transition from traditional silo-based managerial practices to integrated supply chain practices requires drastic changes in organizational structures, cultures, policies, and decision-making processes. Unless such changes were properly managed, the healthcare organization is likely to suffer from miscommunication, role conflicts, frequent bottlenecks, the degrading healthcare worker morale, and the increased resistance to supply chain transformations. In other words, supply chain transformation without prepared change management may defeat the purpose of supply chain initiatives. According to Fries (2005), change management generally comprises three steps:

1. *Unfreezing* that tosses out old ideals and processes to break old habits
2. *Changing* that initiates a new system or major process transformation and creates a team to facilitate the needed transformation throughout the organization
3. *Refreezing* that practices what was implemented, learned, and accepted by the change management team and the impacted organizational units

To elaborate, change management for supply chain transformations may follow the detailed steps described in Table 2.2 (see, e.g., Hughes et al. 1998; NAPM InfoEdge 2000, for supply chain transformations). Since a vision sets the tone for change management, the supply chain vision should be created with input and feedback from all stakeholders including affected healthcare workers. In general, a vision refers to "a picture of the future with some implicit or explicit commentary on what people should

Table 2.2 Change management steps for supply chain transformations

Steps	Action plans	Key points
1	Create visions for stakeholders and supply chain partners and then translate supply chain concepts into their language.	Where are we going? Why? What do we want to accomplish through supply chain transformations? Whom are we partnering with? What are the key supply chain agenda?
2	Develop the change management team and designate change leaders (agents), while mobilizing management commitment to supply chain transformations.	Who will plan the change? Who will lead the change? Who will initiate the change? Can we raise the level of understanding of the need for a change? Are we excited about the change?
3	Create the implementation plan and communicate visions to stakeholders and supply chain partners.	How do we change the current practices? What are we going to do? Who will be responsible for what? Is everyone properly informed? Is everyone on the same page?
4	Develop the initial wave of changes by breaking down the functional silos and then visualize key processes for supply chain transformations.	Where do we begin? Can we create synergies by working together? What are our priorities? Which missions are most critical for the supply chain success? What will it take to make changes?

Table 2.2 (Continued)

5	Identify cost and profit drivers and determine investment priorities.	How much do we have to invest in new supply chain initiatives? What are the sources of expenditures (or financial obligations)? What drives profits? How will the cost and profit be measured?
6	Define performance metrics.	What are deliverables? What is the return-on-investment? How do we assess our progress? What are our benchmarks? Which organizations are our benchmarking targets (or partners)?
7	Develop meaningful incentives and partnering schemes.	How do we share benefits and risks with our supply chain partners?
8	Monitor the current progress.	Do we meet the short-term goals that we set? Are we on the right track?
9	Continue to reengineer supply chain processes.	Can we do better? What needs to be done to improve the current practices?
10	Build-in new ways of doing business in the organizational culture and create new visions.	Do we increase the customer value? Do we improve the bottom line? Are there noticeable cultural changes? How do we stack up against our competitors?

strive to create that future" (Kotter 1996, 68). The vision goes beyond authoritarian decrees and micromanagement to break through all the forces that support the status quo.

2.2.1 Breaking Old Habits in Healthcare Management

In 2011 alone, the U.S. healthcare spending reached three trillion dollar (Munro 2012). However, it does not really matter if much of such spending is wasted and not well utilized. There may be a number of reasons why the U.S. healthcare system is so inefficient. Those reasons may include the following:

1. A *fee-for-service* arrangement for doctors, which encourages them to overtreat and overtest patients with more surgeries, X-rays, and physical examinations.

2. A *fear of malpractice* lawsuit that increases healthcare professionals' insurance burden.

3. Widely *varying prices* of healthcare resulting from a lack of transparency and standardization. Less transparency leads to poor quality of care because patients cannot compare prices with other alternative cares and thus get stuck with a bad option.

4. Disproportionally *high administrative or overhead costs* (e.g., continued use of the paper-based manual system and a large percentage of nonclinical staff) that drive up overall healthcare costs.

5. *Third-party pay* system that encourages both patients and doctors to overuse resources without actual needs because patients cover only a small portion of out-of-pocket expenses, while their employers, insurance companies, governments, and charitable organizations tab most (i.e., three-fourths or higher) of the healthcare bills.

6. *Poor demand planning* that leads to a chronic shortage of essential medical supplies (e.g., intravenous saline bags) or drugs (e.g., flu vaccines), while overstocking other less critical medical necessities (e.g., nutritional supplements) or slow-moving items.

7. Lack of focus on *preventive care* (e.g., reduction in a patient's cholesterol level and weight control preventing obesity).

Although all the sources of healthcare inefficiencies listed earlier cannot be eliminated at once without a series of radical healthcare reforms and policy changes, some of them can be tackled by changing old bad habits with the adaptation of supply chain principles.

2.2.2 Initiating Change

Realizing the negative consequences of old bad habits, we need to make changes in what we have done in the past. Although sources of healthcare inefficiency varied as illustrated in the previous subsection, those sources are tied with traditional healthcare practices that are more provider-driven or payor-driven in that healthcare providers and payors (e.g., insurance companies) set the stage for pricing and the extent of treatments. That is to say, patients (ultimate customers) are not in charge of their own healthcare and have no control over their choices of healthcare providers and needed services. Since they are not allowed to comparison-shop and then select the best available care, providers have no incentive to offer competitive price and services for their patients. As such, some experts such as Herzlinger (2002) proposed that making the healthcare industry more patient-centric would be the best way to change the old bad habit. Using the conventional wisdom, if a patient stays at the hospital for an extra day per his or her doctor's instruction against his or her desire since his or her medical bill for an extra care will be covered by the insurer, it not only creates moral hazard but also creates potential inefficiency. For instance, Robbins et al. (1994) argued that healthcare inefficiencies were mainly caused by too much third-party payment of medical bills and too much insurance coverage. Regardless of a dispute over the potential harm (e.g., wasteful spending) or gain (e.g., patient welfare) of such extra care from an economic standpoint, the influx of patient-centric mentality into the healthcare system will take time. In light of the preceding discussions, some immediate and plausible remedies are needed to jump-start changes in old bad habits. These remedies include the following:

1. *Healthcare reengineering* that helps healthcare organizations reorder their priorities, redesign healthcare functions (e.g., administrative processes), and consolidate overlapping healthcare deliveries to create societal value for patients. It should be driven by what the patient wants and what the healthcare market needs. Accelerated alignment of clinical and management processes, systems integration, and healthcare process redesign are cores of this reengineering effort (Boland 1996; Lin and Vassar 1996).

2. *Total quality management (TQM)* can be an integral part of reengineering efforts because it helps the healthcare organization delve into the wasteful sources (e.g., medical error, avoidable readmissions of patients, slow lab turnaround time, claim reimbursement red-tapes, and distribution bottlenecks) of the current practices. TQM reflects the needs of patients rather than the vested interests and rights of providers by involving all the healthcare stakeholders in the continuous process improvement efforts.

3. *Information exchange and sharing* among healthcare partners that improves transparency and visibility throughout the healthcare

delivery processes. For example, unless patient privacy is violated, a timely transmission of clinical information (including medical records) about a patient to his or her provider (e.g., doctor) will improve the efficiency of patient treatment and care. A study conducted by Walker et al. (2005) revealed that standardized healthcare information exchange and interoperability could yield a net value of $77.8 billion per year once it was fully implemented. More importantly, a majority of both patients and healthcare providers believed that the benefits of patient information sharing would outweigh its drawbacks (Perera et al. 2011).

2.2.3 Refreezing the Proven Best Practices

Regardless of potential benefits, the efforts to change one's old habits (e.g., behavior, attitude, and value) usually face strong resistance from a number of people within the organization and its partners. To implement the planned change such as the adoption of supply chain principles without various organization hurdles (including internal politics), one should first communicate to affected parties (e.g., healthcare workers and trading partners) about the need for a change, the benefits from a change, the barriers to overcome, and the rewards and incentives for the people involved in the change management process. Since a change will bring a new set of values and the subsequent new performance standards, the establishment of a new performance evaluation and reward system should be a priority for change management. Once the performance appraisal standards are set and a new reward system is in place, the healthcare organization needs to provide its stakeholders (especially employees) with the clear guidance of which steps must be taken to implement a new way of doing things. Such guidance can be obtained from the other peers' successful best-in-class practices. In the healthcare sector, the following illustrates some of those practices.

1. *Mass customization* through *precision medicine* that examines the individual's disease vulnerability using genomics and focuses on preventive care for a disease susceptible population cluster (e.g., patients with a diabetic heritage) in a proactive manner.

2. *Health informatics* that utilizes advanced information and communication technology to transmit, store, save, and share patient information (e.g., treatment history, lab test results, and genomic profiles) throughout the healthcare supply chain with a goal of creating *one-patient, one-record* databases. This will prevent redundancy and confusion, while shortening patient response time.

3. *Integrated care* that brings together inputs, delivery, management, and organization of healthcare services as a means of improving access, quality, user satisfaction, and efficiency (Gröne and Garcia-Barbero 2001). As shown in Figure 2.1, integrated care aims to coordinate and synchronize various types of interdependent healthcare services to maximize the patient welfare and safety and the subsequent patient satisfaction by combining the resources of healthcare providers and insurers.

2.3   Strategic Alliances among Healthcare Partners

To create synergy resultant from the integration of healthcare functions and processes, a healthcare organization needs to make conscious efforts to forge strategic alliances (or partnership) with other peer organizations

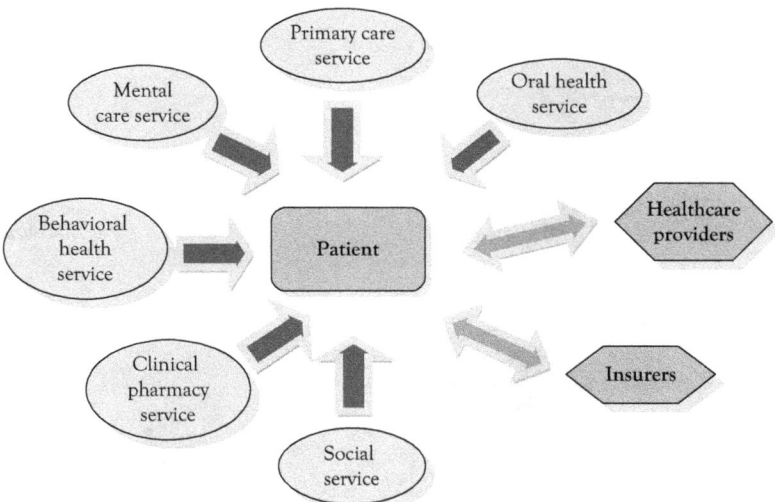

Figure 2.1 The basic integrated care model

or trading partners throughout the supply chain. However, interorganizational alliances were often plagued by ambiguities in the level of commitments (or responsibilities) from each partner, a lack of mutual trust between partners and the subsequent lack of information exchange and sharing, imbalances in the channel power and risk sharing, and differences in organizational culture and strategic focus. To cope with these challenges, healthcare organizations entering into strategic alliances or partnership should understand where they can find partners, what kind of partnership they are forming, what kind of role each partner should play, and how they should build and manage a partnership. The following subsections will explain the details of enhancing such understanding.

2.3.1   Finding Right Partners

As displayed in Figure 2.2, the first step for building strategic alliances or partnerships is to find right partners. Although the meaning of right may vary from one organization to another, a *right partner* in the supply chain context generally refers to an organization that shares the vision for achieving its strategic goals, is willing to offer the fair share of resources (including expertise), and is unlikely to exploit the alliance to its own ends or self-interests (e.g., just cost- or risk-sharing options and knowhow

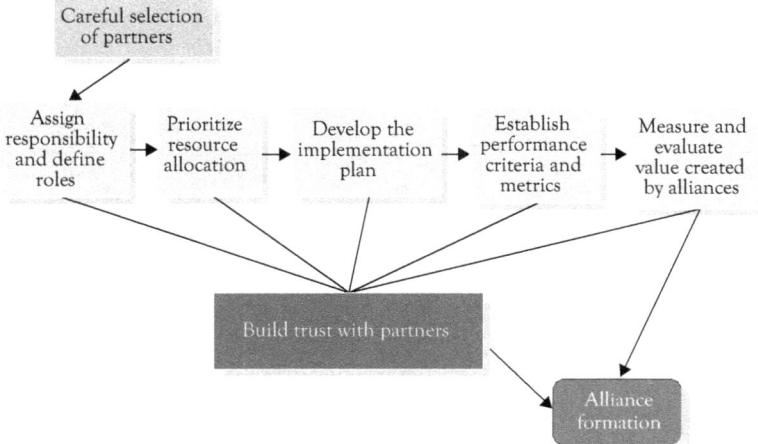

Figure 2.2 Steps for building strategic alliances

or technology transfer). In particular, a right partner should exhibit both organizational and technical compatibility. Organizational compatibility means the organization's adaptability to its partner's value propositions, beliefs, philosophy, and relationship in terms of organizational culture. Technical compatibility indicates the organization's flexibility or readiness to adopt new information technology (e.g., electronic data interchange and radio frequency identification) that will facilitate communication and the subsequent cooperation between aligned partners. Also, to sustain the long-term partnership, the healthcare organization should examine the complementarity (e.g., care givers and long-term care providers) and interdependency (e.g., intravenous solution producers and surgical units, and emergency care providers and ambulance operators) of two aligned organizations.

2.3.2   Organizational Learning through Partnerships

One of the most important benefits of forming strategic alliances is the increased opportunity to learn new idea, knowhow, and technology from alliance partners. This learning opportunity also includes the sharing of knowledge about patient needs, market forces, industry dynamics, and innovative practices from their alliance partners. Thus, one of the incentives for forming strategic alliances among supply chain partners would be organizational learning. In a broad sense, organizational learning is a process of increasing the organizational capacity for more efficient and effective organizational actions through knowledge sharing and constructive dialogue (Fiol and Lyles 1985; Garvin 2000; Bell et al. 2002). That process is typically made of a repetitive cycle of actions such as education and training, improving, discovering, sharing, and communicating with alliance partners, as shown in Figure 2.3. Specifically, education, training, and repetitive experiences lead to expertise that improves decision outcomes and then enhances reputation (Carroll and Edmonson 2002). Enhanced reputation can not only attract more patients, but also increase the chance of more partnership opportunities with other healthcare organizations that aspire to improve their performances with learned knowledge, skills, and technology. A key to the success of organizational learning effort includes knowledge creation and dissemination through

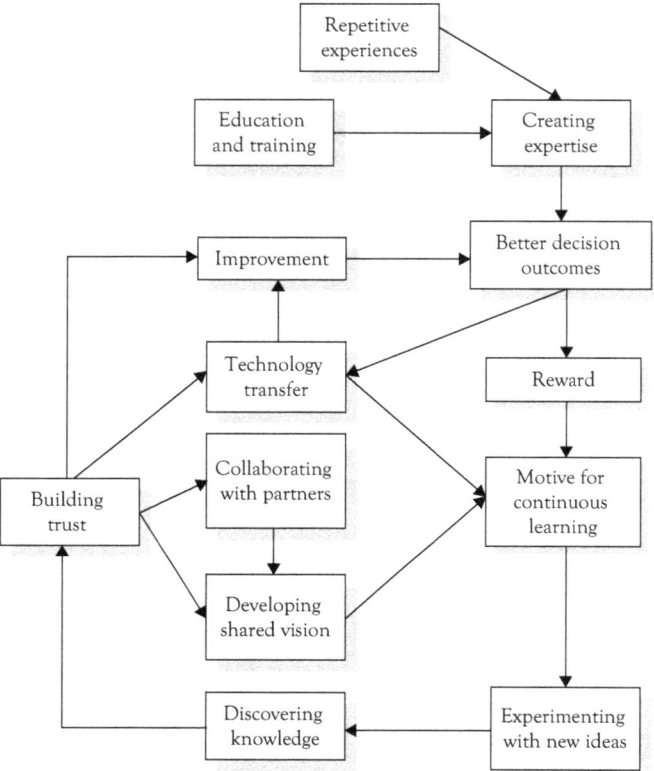

Figure 2.3 The illustrated organizational learning process

uninterrupted information flows throughout healthcare processes and the entire supply chain. The knowledge passed on to the partners, in turn, helps create shared goals and vision that create synergies for improving the healthcare productivity.

Organizational learning consists of knowledge acquisition, dissemination, and shared interpretation of knowledge across the organizations (Sinkula 1994; Min 2001). The knowledge that can be gained from other organizations is of two types:

1. *Explicit* knowledge that can be codified and easily transmitted to partnering organizations. Its examples are knowledge often captured

in the forms of documented texts, tables, figures, diagrams, scientific formulas, standards, and written performance metrics (Nonaka 1991).

2. *Tacit* knowledge that cannot be easily communicated to partnering organizations due to its implicit, noncodifiable context. Its examples include technical expertise and job-specific insights possessed by ambulance dispatchers, airplane pilots, ocean vessel navigators, insurance underwriters, and logistics engineers.

Organizational learning can occur at two different levels of the decision making hierarchy: operational and strategic (see, e.g., Fiol and Lyles 1985; Sinkula 1994).

1. *Operational learning* that allows partnering organizations to improve their day-to-day practices and policies through the mutual detection and correction of errors and inefficient operations.

2. *Strategic learning* that allows partnering organizations to redefine their overall missions, strategies, goals, and philosophies through the development of innovative thoughts and ideas.

Regardless of the type of organizational learning, the extent and effectiveness of organizational learning may be greatly influenced by the level of trust between partnering organizations. Without mutual trust, organizations in the supply chain may be unwilling to share their information and consequently reluctant to diffuse their innovations and technology to their supply chain partners. Thus, it is important to build trust among supply chain partners before forming strategic alliances and then exploiting the opportunity to learn from each other. Indeed, the recent study conducted by Kwon and Suh (2004) indicated that the presence of trust greatly improved supply chain performances. On the other hand, a lack of trust among supply chain partners often resulted in inefficient and ineffective performance as the transaction costs increased. Also, organizational learning can be enhanced when efforts are led by highly skilled, full-time managers who take the leadership in encouraging innovation and focus on creating opportunities for learning (Reay et al. 2009).

In the healthcare sector, organizational learning can be used to enhance patient safety and quality improvement in medical practices. For instance, a creation of the shared database of medical errors (including prescription mistakes, misdiagnosis) and documented evidences of underlying sources of those errors may facilitate learning from past mistakes and thus help healthcare organizations obviate future errors and improve their quality of care. Similarly, some administrative errors such as medical billing error can be reduced by following the organizational learning process described earlier.

CHAPTER 3

Designing Sustainable Healthcare Supply Chains

Any human activity consumes natural resources such as air, water, minerals, and natural sources (e.g., wind, geothermal, and solar power) of energy and can consequently do harm to our natural environments that produce resources. To continuously use natural resources for a number of generations to come, human species should find a way to regenerate those resources by maintaining the ecological balances of natural environments. In this regard, healthcare process is no exception. For example, to treat sick or injured patients, doctors have to use medicines that are made of natural herbs and chemical ingredients extracted from natural sources. Also, to operate medical equipment (e.g., X-ray machine) and maintain healthcare facilities (e.g., hospitals and medical labs), a healthcare organization has to use utilities (e.g., electricity) that originate from fossil fuel, water, or wind. If humans fail to renew and recreate natural resources, human activities including healthcare activities will stop. As such, it is very important for the healthcare organization to be conscious of sustainability. Sustainability often connotes environmental protection and preservation. However, it means far more than conserving natural environments, reducing waste, and cleaning air. *Sustainability* is about developing an ecologically aware, socially just, and economically responsible society (Students for Sustainability 2014).

With this mind, the next sections will discuss about ways to enhance sustainability of healthcare processes in the supply chain by identifying the root causes of sustainability problems in healthcare and then creating some potential remedies.

3.1   Understanding Patient Expectations and Perceptions of Healthcare Services

If we waste resources by producing unnecessary products and rendering unwanted services, we will consume resources more than we need to and consequently have to make more effort than usual to regenerate wasted resources. In other words, wasted resources resulting from a poor understanding of customer demand are the main sources of sustainability problems. Therefore, sustainability efforts should begin with a clear understanding of what the customer (patient) needs, wants, and desires. To better understand customers (patients), the hospital organization has to listen to them, empathize with them, and customize healthcare for them. Since patient demand (e.g., need) may vary from one patient to another, the development of patient profiles seems to be the first step toward patient understanding. To develop accurate profiles of patients, the hospital organization needs to segment its patient bases and then constantly listen to them by creating a communication channel through patient relationship management. The next subsections will discuss about the details of patient segmentation and patient relationship management.

3.1.1   *Segmenting Target Patient Bases*

The best way to understand a patient's specific needs and cater healthcare services to those needs is to segment patient bases with respect to the patient's demographic profile (e.g., gender, age, and occupation), geographic location (e.g., warm- or cold-weather region), economic status (e.g., income level and purchasing power), life style (e.g., active or sedentary), insurance coverage, medical condition, and vulnerability to a certain disease (e.g., obese people with a greater likelihood of heart disease and diabetes). An example of the patient segmentation model that classifies patients into their medical condition categories is a *pyramid* diagram model displayed in Figure 3.1. This diagram model illustrates what level of medical attention or intervention care is needed to better serve patients based on their specific medical conditions (or illness burdens) that were categorized by Moore (2012).

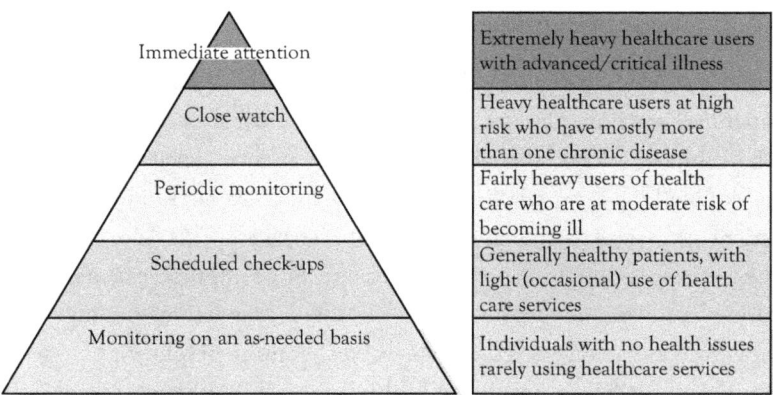

Figure 3.1 A pyramid of the patient segmentation with respect to illness burden

Generally speaking, patient segmentation is considered an essential element of patient-centric customization processes that break down heterogeneous patient bases into a smaller number of homogeneous subgroups, in response to different characteristics, needs, preferences, and desires of patients. For instance, Dranove et al. (1993) observed that privately insured patients had a tendency to go to hospitals offering more comprehensive healthcare services, while Hispanic patients tended to go to low-cost hospitals, ceteris paribus. As such, hospitals that have many privately insured patients need to focus on high quality care rather than cost of care, while hospitals that primarily target Hispanic populations should be aware of their patients' sensitivity to pricing. Likewise, to better serve diabetic patients by creating early warning signals, the hospital may ensure the constant supplies of pocket-size blood glucose monitors and exploit them for their health monitoring.

As discussed earlier, patient segmentation can not only help the healthcare organization improve its patient satisfaction, but also help reduce wasteful spending and efforts by allocating resources to the areas of services exactly patients want. For example, after the INTEGRIS Health, a large healthcare system in Oklahoma with 14 hospitals successfully implemented a patient segmentation strategy (e.g., patient segmentation based on payment likelihood); their organization had virtually eliminated all customer service complaints related to their financial experiences such as medical billing (Eller 2009).

3.1.2 Patient Relationship Management

Interaction with patients is increasingly being recognized as a key to patient satisfaction, because it will increase the comfort level of patients for healthcare. Thus, the idea of recognizing most loyal patients and developing long-term relationships with them is essential to high-quality patient care and sustainable healthcare services. This idea typically involves responding to the patient's request for prompt treatments, monitoring the patient's progress after necessary treatments, dealing with patient queries and complaints expeditiously, and then following up with the patient on his or her future healthcare needs. Although the idea of patient relationship management (PRM) is similar to that of customer relationship management (CRM) in the business world in that both ideas arose from the increasing emphasis on service recipients (customer or patients), the former is somewhat different from the latter in that patient relations are more constrained or locked-up than customer relations in the business world. For example, physicians are not necessarily obligated to treat every patient and thus can refuse to provide care for some patients, unless a legal patient–physician relationship (with the presence of an express agreement by the physician to treat a patient) was established prior to request for care. It is a well-known fact that many physicians refuse to treat new patients, regardless of patients' medical urgency. On the other hand, business entities are required to serve any customers who ask for services or products. Also, the PRM values patient privacy far more than the CRM values customer privacy.

Though the PRM concept seems to be still elusive based on the preceding discussions, patient relationship management (PRM) can be defined as a core healthcare strategy that intends to attract, retain, and nurture patients by building social bonds with them, securing their trust or loyalty, and providing highest possible value to them through constant dialogues and engagements. PRM often targets so-called loyal patients who repeatedly come back to the same healthcare provider and can give referrals to other potential patients. Reaching out to those targeted patients, PRM may exploit information and communication technology (ICT) that help the healthcare provider gain insights into patient behavior and value. PRM can bring a lot of benefits to both patients and their healthcare providers. These benefits include the following:

1. More informed decisions by the healthcare provider and the subsequent reduction in misdiagnosis and medical error through more frequent information sharing (e.g., medical history and treatment records) between the patient and his or her healthcare provider
2. Personalized care through mutual understanding of the patient's expectations of the healthcare provider and the healthcare provider's expectations of the patient
3. Avoiding costly disputes (e.g., malpractice lawsuits) with patients through improved personal rapport with them (Beckman et al. 1994)
4. Increased patient satisfaction and more word-of-mouth referrals from loyal patients to potential new patients (Oinas-Kukkonen et al. 2008)

3.1.3 Healthcare Service Audits

The main goals of a healthcare service audit are to ensure efficient and effective delivery of high-quality healthcare, to check whether the systematic healthcare procedures are in place, and to continuously improve the financial health of the healthcare provider by eliminating the sources of nonvalue-adding services and preventing medical errors, frauds, and abuses. The healthcare service audits may involve: (1) the evaluation of the current level of healthcare services from internal perspectives; (2) the appraisal of the impact of healthcare services on the healthcare provider's brand recognition and productivity; and (3) the benchmark of healthcare service performances relative to the healthcare provider's peers (including rivals). Prior to evaluating the existing healthcare service, a service audit should begin with the development of clear service objectives, formulation of service plans, and establishment of reporting channels (Lambert and Lewis 1980). A key to the success of healthcare service audits is maintaining the accuracy and timeliness of information obtained from patient feedback, suggestions of healthcare professionals or workers (e.g., doctors and nurses), and peer evaluations. Common target areas of audits include the following:

- Duplicated and redundant test procedures
- Bundling healthcare services
- Unauthorized, unapproved services

- Slow responses to patient requests for doctor's appointments and treatments
- Retrospective reviews of patient charts after patient discharge
- Outliers in billing and payment indicating potential fraudulent claims
- Unbilled, unsupported, and undocumented charges
- Procure-to-pay processes (including tax compliances for purchased goods or services)
- Recording, coding, or documentation error in electronic health record (HER)
- Reimbursement deficiencies
- Compliances with federal certification requirements
- Compliances with regulatory requirements such as the Health Insurance Portability and Accountability Act (HIPAA), Affordable Care Act (ACA), and Food and Drug Administration (FDA) rules
- Any practices that may draw attention from governmental investigational auditors such as recovery audit contractors (RACs) or zone program integrity contractors (ZPICs)

As illustrated earlier, the audit can target a number of different areas. These areas can be categorized into three different types: (1) performance, (2) process, and (3) physical environmental audits. *Performance audit* refers to an evaluation of healthcare service outcomes after the service was rendered to the patient group. Such outcomes may include: patient mortality, readmission rates, a length of hospital stay, and a frequency of patient complaints. *Process audit* checks and sees whether current work flows contribute to the improvement of healthcare value and productivity. Process audit examines who does what tasks, in what sequence, and what purposes to weed out unnecessary tasks and arrange tasks in seamless sequence. *Physical environmental audit* investigates the relevance and functionality of physical infrastructure (e.g., medical equipment, lab facility, hospital beds, ambulances, and information systems) to see if it plays its intended role in healthcare service delivery. These three types of audits can be conducted retrospectively, concurrently, and prospectively.

3.2   Delivering Healthcare

There are a number of different ways patients can be treated depending on their medical condition, urgency of care, and insurance coverage. The way patients are treated is directly tied to a manner in which healthcare service is delivered to the patients. To elaborate, the decision as to how patients should be treated usually dictates in which location (e.g., hospital versus home) patient care will take place, in which channel (e.g., primary versus auxiliary care) patient care will be provided, and what healthcare provider (e.g., generalist versus specialist) will be responsible for patient care. In other words, such a decision sets the stage for the healthcare delivery process and thus can have a profound impact on quality of care. Considering the importance of healthcare delivery to quality of care, the following subsections will introduce its fundamental concepts and discuss ways to enhance healthcare delivery systems.

3.2.1   Inpatient, Outpatient, and Urgent Care

The main goals of a healthcare delivery system are increasing patient access to quality care while keeping the cost of care under control. To achieve these goals, the healthcare organization should decide on the manner in which healthcare resources are utilized without waste while ensuring most accessible, highest quality healthcare services. That decision involves selecting the proper type and setting of care for each patient and allocating right resources (including human resources such as medical professionals) to the treatment of that particular patient. Table 3.1 summarizes various types of healthcare delivery services and their appropriate settings. In a broad sense, these types can be classified into three categories: (1) inpatient, (2) outpatient, and (3) urgent care. These categories can be further divided into six subcategories as recapitulated in Table 3.1. Herein, *primary care* typically addresses the wide range of healthcare issues including acute, chronic, and preventive healthcare issues as the initial point of consultation related to the patient's symptoms or healthcare concerns. A primary care provider (e.g., family physician) often gives patients referrals for secondary or tertiary care and coordinates specialty care when needed. *Secondary care* focuses on health problems associated with a specific organ (e.g., eyes, ears, and heart) and particular disease (e.g., diabetes, cancers,

Table 3.1 Healthcare types and their relevant setting

	Examples of institutions	Examples of healthcare professionals
Primary care	Doctor's offices, clinics, schools, prisons, mobile vans	Family physicians, nurse practitioners, physician assistants, pediatricians, obstetricians, gynecologists
Secondary care	Community hospitals, specialty (e.g., cancer) clinics, diagnostic imaging labs, magnetic resonance imaging labs, intensive care units	Internists, cardiologists, oncologists, ophthalmologists, endocrinologists, dermatologists, geriatricians, orthodontists, neurosurgeons, orthopedic surgeons, psychiatrists
Tertiary care	Regional medical centers, medical schools, burn centers, birthing centers	Specialists, medical researchers, occupational therapists
Preventive care	Public health organizations, wellness and fitness centers, pharmacies	Chiropractors, fitness instructors, clinical dieticians, epidemiologists
Outpatient care	Nursing homes, assisted living facilities, outpatient surgical centers, rehabilitative centers	Hospices, care givers, nurses
Emergency (urgent) care	General hospitals, satellite clinics, ambulances, trauma centers	Paramedics, ER doctors

and thyroid). *Tertiary care* refers to a specialized consultative care over an extended period of time, usually on referral from primary or secondary care providers. Tertiary care requires a state-of-art facility, highly specialized equipment, and medical expertise in highly advanced subfields such as coronary artery bypass surgery, renal hemodialysis, neurosurgery, movement disorder, multiple sclerosis, and severe burn treatments.

Since hospitals generally operate fully for about five or six hours a day and doctors are not supposed to attend to 10 patients an hour, outpatient service makes sense (Parvatiyar and Sheth 2001). *Outpatient care* refers to medical care, test, or treatment that does not require more than 24 hours of hospitalization (i.e., an overnight stay) in a medical facility (e.g., hospital and clinic). Outpatient care includes: (1) wellness and prevention, such as weight-loss programs; (2) diagnosis, such as lab tests and MRI scans; (3) treatment, such as minor surgeries and chemotherapy; and (4) rehabilitation, such as drug or alcohol rehab and physical therapy (WebMD 2011). *Emergency care* handles the patient's acute medical conditions. Emergency (urgent) care is one of the most challenged parts of healthcare delivery due to extreme time-sensitivity of treatments requiring little margin for error. In this care, a patient can arrive through multiple channels (walk-in, drive-in, or ambulance) and meet with the receptionist for background checks and admission. Afterward, the patient is stabilized and prioritized for immediate care and then treated by the ER doctor and nurse after going through a series of medical tests (e.g., X-rays, CT scan, and MRI). Once emergency treatments are completed, the patient will be admitted to the hospital. Unlike other cares, emergency care should avoid any overcrowding, prolonged delays of tests and treatments, medical staff shortages, and a lack of on-call specialists. *Preventive care* intends to protect, promote, and sustain the health and well-being of population sectors that are vulnerable to a certain disease, disability, and death. Examples of preventive care include: immunization vaccination, colorectal cancer screening via colonoscopy, cholesterol level control, HIV test for sexually transmitted diseases, monitoring high blood pressure, treatments for alcohol, tobacco, or substance abuse, weight control, diet and nutrition counseling, mammography screening (film and digital) for all adult women, genetic screening and evaluation, cervical cancer screening including Pap smears, and the use of prophylactic antibiotics preventing diarrhea. In contrast with other healthcare deliveries gearing toward the treatment of illness after the fact (after the acute symptom shows), preventive care can not only save the high expenditures of curative care but also obviate debilitating or painful symptoms.

3.2.2   Access to Healthcare Services

Healthcare cannot be delivered to patients unless they can get access to it. Indeed, according to the Gallop Poll, 30 percent of surveyed Americans believed that healthcare access was the biggest concern for healthcare delivery services (Jones 2008). To increase healthcare access, the healthcare provider should remove geographical (distance), financial, social, or communication barriers for prospective patients. For example, according to the National Health Interview Survey conducted by the Centers for Disease Control and Prevention, the percentage of Americans of all ages who had a usual place to go for healthcare is 86.8 percent in 2011 (CDC 2012). This means that the remaining 14 percent of Americans have no place to go for needed healthcare, if their health problems arise. In particular, more than a quarter (26.9 percent) of young adult Americans with an age group of 18 to 24 had no place to go for healthcare. Although 9.2 percent of those aged 18 to 64 attributed their healthcare access problems to cost, cost alone cannot be a hindrance to their healthcare access (CDC 2012). Given that many sick people are physically impaired, traveling long distances to healthcare facilities creates another formidable barrier for their healthcare access. This problem can be compounded in the rural area where medical doctors are few and healthcare facilities are scattered. The next two subsections will focus on the discussion of physical healthcare access issues.

3.2.3   Healthcare Facility Location

The *environment of care*—physical environments (e.g., building, equipment, and internal design) in which healthcare is provided—can impact the quality of care because it may limit or expand the doctor's capacity to treat patients and the patient's comfort level. For example, if the medical building does not meet required sanitary conditions and harbors germs, it will threaten patient safety. Similarly, if the medical facility is not equipped with the functioning medical equipment such as the computer topology (CT) scanner or runs out of medical isotopes for medical testing, the doctor will face a difficulty in finding the real source of the patient's medical problem and thus cannot diagnose or treat the patient in a timely manner. However, even if there exists a healthcare facility with desirable environment of care, its physical distance from the patient's residence or workplace can influence how often such a facility will be utilized by the patient and subsequently how efficiently healthcare services will be delivered to that patient. As such, healthcare facility location matters most for healthcare access.

Recognizing the significant role of healthcare facility in the quality of care, the healthcare facility location problem is one of the most highly researched subjects in healthcare planning. This line of research was led by Schultz (1970) and Calvo and Marks (1973). healthcare facility location planning is primarily concerned with the optimal number, size, and location-allocation of healthcare facilities that can maximize healthcare access while minimizing costs. Three types of basic mathematical models and their variations are commonly used to tackle the healthcare facility location problems. These three basic models are: (1) set covering model; (2) maximal covering model; and (3) p-median model that aimed to enhance accessibility, adaptability, and the availability of healthcare (Daskin and Dean 2004).

To elaborate, the set covering model attempts to minimize the cost of healthcare facilities that are selected so that all patient demand nodes are covered (Chvatal 1979). It is mathematically expressed as follows:

Minimize
$$\sum_{j \in J} c_j x_j \qquad (1)$$

Subject to:
$$\sum_{j \in J} a_{ij} x_j \geq 1 \quad \forall i \in I \qquad (2)$$

$$x_j \in \{0,1\} \quad \forall j \in J \qquad (3)$$

where $a_{ij} = \begin{cases} 1, \text{ if demand } i \text{ can be covered by a healthcare facility at} \\ \quad \text{potential site } j \\ 0, \text{ otherwise} \end{cases}$

$x_j = \begin{cases} 1, \text{ if a healthcare facility is located at site } j \\ 0, \text{ otherwise} \end{cases}$

c_j = cost of locating a healthcare facility at potential site j

I = a set of patient demand i

J = a set of potential site j

In the preceding equations, the objective function (1) minimizes the total cost of locating all the chosen healthcare facilities. Constraint (2) ensures that each demand node must be covered by at least one of the chosen facilities. Constraint (3) is binary integrality requirements.

The maximum covering model seeks to maximize the population (potential patients) who can be served within a stated service distance or time given a limited number of healthcare facilities (Church and ReVelle 1974). Its mathematical formulation can be stated as follows:

Maximize
$$\sum_{i \in I} a_i y_i \qquad (4)$$

Subject to:
$$\sum_{j \in N_i} x_j \geq y_i \quad \forall i \in I \qquad (5)$$

$$\sum_{j \in J} x_j = P \qquad (6)$$

$$x_j \in \{0,1\} \quad \forall j \in J \qquad (7)$$

$$y_i \in \{0,1\} \quad \forall i \in I \qquad (8)$$

where a_i = population (potential patients) to be served at demand node i

$y_i = \begin{cases} 1, \text{ if demand node } i \text{ is covered} \\ 0, \text{ otherwise} \end{cases}$

$x_j = \begin{cases} 1, \text{ if a healthcare facility is opened at site } j \\ 0, \text{ otherwise} \end{cases}$

P = a number of healthcare facilities to be located

S = a distance beyond which a demand point is considered "uncovered." The value of S can be chosen differently for each demand point, if desired.

d_{ij} = the shortest distance from node i to node j

$N_i = \{ j \in J \,|\, d_{ij} \leq S \}$

The objective function (4) maximizes the coverage of healthcare demands. Constraint (5) states that demand node i cannot be counted as covered unless we locate at least one healthcare facility that is able to cover the demand node. Constraint (6) states that the exact designated number of healthcare facilities is to be located. Constraints (7) and (8) are binary integrality requirements.

The p-median model intends to find a set of healthcare facilities that should be available for services and to determine which population groups (patients) should be served from which facilities, so that the travel costs of serving all the healthcare demand from all chosen facilities can be minimized (Tansel et al. 1983). Its formulation is as follows:

Minimize $$\sum_{i \in I} \sum_{j \in J} w_i d_{ij} y_{ij} \qquad (9)$$

Subject to: $$\sum_{j \in J} y_{ij} = 1 \qquad \forall i \in I \qquad (10)$$

$$y_{ij} \le x_j \qquad \forall i \in I, \forall j \in J \qquad (11)$$

$$\sum_{j \in J} x_j = P \qquad (12)$$

$$x_j \in \{0,1\} \qquad \forall j \in J \qquad (13)$$

$$y_{ij} \in \{0,1\} \qquad \forall i \in I, \forall j \in J \qquad (14)$$

where w_j = weight given to projected demand
d_{ij} = a distance from demand node i to site j
$y_{ij} = \begin{cases} 1, \text{ if patient demand at node } i \text{ is allocated to healthcare} \\ \quad \text{facility at site } j \\ 0, \text{ otherwise} \end{cases}$

The objective function (9) minimizes the demand weighted total distance or total travel cost. This objective function can be viewed as a proxy for the maximization of accessibility of the healthcare facilities. Constraint (10) states that each demand node must be assigned to exactly one facility site and thus all demands should be fully served by the facility. Constraint (11) stipulates that demand nodes can only be assigned to open (available) facility sites. Constraint (12) ensures that the exact designated number of healthcare facilities is to be located. Constraints (13) and (14) are binary integrality requirements. But, it is noted that constraint (14) can be relaxed to a simple nonnegativity constraint (i.e., $0 \le y_{ij} \le 1$) since each demand node can be assigned to the closest open healthcare facility.

3.2.4 Emergency Vehicle Deployment

Between 2001 and 2009, annual emergency care admissions in the United States increased by 79 percent from 1.2 to 2.2 million (Herring et al. 2013). An increase in emergency care actually outpaced the population growth in the United States during that time span. Especially, senior citizens accounted for 156 million emergency department visits in the United States from 2001 to 2009 (Pines et al. 2013). With a graying population trend and a greater number of incidents in natural disasters (e.g., Hurricane Katrina and Sandy), there is no sign of abatement in demand for emergency care. An increase in emergency care means a greater likelihood of emergency vehicle (ambulance) deployment. That is to say, emergency vehicle deployment planning will be an important part of healthcare delivery systems. Typically, emergency vehicle deployment planning involves determining how many emergency vehicles are needed, where emergency vehicles should be stationed to equitably serve both high-demand (metropolitan) and low-demand (rural) areas, at what times they should operate, what mode (e.g., van versus helicopter) of emergency vehicles should be selected, which emergency vehicles should cover which geographical areas, and what specific vehicle dispatch policy (e.g., communication channels and protocols, and back-up plans) should be employed. Considering the inherent complexity of emergency vehicle deployment planning, some analytical tools such as operations research (OR), simulation, and a geographical information system (GIS) were frequently used. Examples of popular OR techniques include variations of set covering and maximal covering location models introduced earlier (e.g., Fitzsimmons 1973; Daskin and Stern 1981; Eaton et al. 1985; Brotcorne et al. 2003; Goldberg 2004). Among these, one of the most useful models that take into account the unpredictable, random natures of emergency care is the maximum expected covering location model that can be mathematically stated (Daskin 1983; ReVelle 1989):

Maximize
$$\sum_{i \in I} \sum_{k=1}^{n_i} (1-q)(q^{k-1}) a_i y_{ik} \qquad (15)$$

Subject to:
$$\sum_{k=1}^{n_i} y_{ik} \le \sum_{j \in N_j} x_j \qquad \forall i \in I \qquad (16)$$

$$\sum_{j\in J} x_j = p \tag{17}$$

$$y_{ik} \in \{0,1\} \quad \forall i \in I, \forall k \in n_i \tag{18}$$

$$x_j \text{ is a positive integer } (x_j \geq 0) \quad \forall j \in J \tag{19}$$

where $y_{ik} = \begin{cases} 1, \text{if emergency demand at node } i \text{ is covered by emergency} \\ \quad \text{vehicle } k \\ 0, \text{otherwise} \end{cases}$

x_j = a number of available (not busy) emergency vehicles stationed at site j

a_i = a population (potential patients) at demand node i

n_i = a number of available emergency vehicles within N_i

N_i = a geographical range of an emergency vehicle stations that can cover emergency demand at node i

q = "busy" probability that all available emergency vehicles within N_i are busy

p = a predesignated number of emergency vehicles

In the preceding model formulation, objective function (15) maximizes the coverage of total expected emergency demand. Constraint (16) stipulates that emergency demand will be covered only when a nearby emergency vehicle is not busy. Constraint (17) limits the number of emergency vehicles to be deployed. Constraint (18) is a binary integrality requirement for y_{ik}. Constraint (19) prohibits the negativity of x_j.

3.3   Sourcing Medical Equipment and Supplies

Medical equipment, devices, and supplies are resources most critical to healthcare delivery services. Imagine that a surgical unit in the hospital runs out of syringes, infusion pumps, sterilizers, defibrillators, respiratory ventilators, surgical microscopes, surgical headlights, anesthesia vaporizers, suction pumps, or any other operating room equipment and supplies, when the patient suffering from acute trauma arrives at the hospital. Without them, the patient cannot be diagnosed, treated, and monitored by doctors and thus may lose his or her life. As such, the healthcare provider should ensure that these resources (assets) are always functional, safe, timely replenished, and then properly configured and maintained to meet healthcare quality standards without glitches. On the other hand, stockpiling too much of these assets beyond healthcare needs can be a main source of waste and inefficiency. Considering this challenging dilemma, the healthcare provider needs to develop a careful plan of managing these assets. Such a plan begins with a formulation of purchasing strategies related to the acquisition of essential medical equipment, devices, and supplies.

Prior to developing these purchasing strategies, one should understand fundamental differences between medical asset purchasing and industrial purchasing in profit-making companies. To elaborate, the cost containment pressure for acquiring medical assets is not as high as that for capital equipment in the business sector. The rationale being that the availability of essential medical equipment is a matter of the patient's life and death and thus this sense of urgency may force the healthcare provider to skip standard acquisition procedures and buy that equipment at a higher price without much negotiation leverage. Also, since ultimate healthcare payors are not necessarily patients but their insurers or government entities, the healthcare provider may be more tolerant of a higher price tag of medical equipment. Also, in contrast with typical industrial purchasing situations, there is a limited number of medical equipment and supply producers due to the unique and customized nature of medical assets (e.g., pace maker for a health disease patient). For example, three defibrillator makers (Phillips HeartStart, Cardiac Science, and Physio-Control) are dominant in the U.S. market. These are all located in the Seattle metro area. Similarly, there are only three viable suppliers of intravenous saline: Baxter Healthcare, B. Braun Medica, and Hospira. Given the limited sources of supply illustrated earlier, it will be harder for the healthcare provider to gain negotiation leverage for lower pricing. This is the reason why a Group Purchasing Organization (GPO) comes into play for the acquisition of essential medical equipment and supplies. GPO not only increases purchasing power, but also reduces sourcing risk for membership organizations by prescreening substandard suppliers. In general, medical asset purchasing procedures comprise 10 steps shown in Figure 3.2.

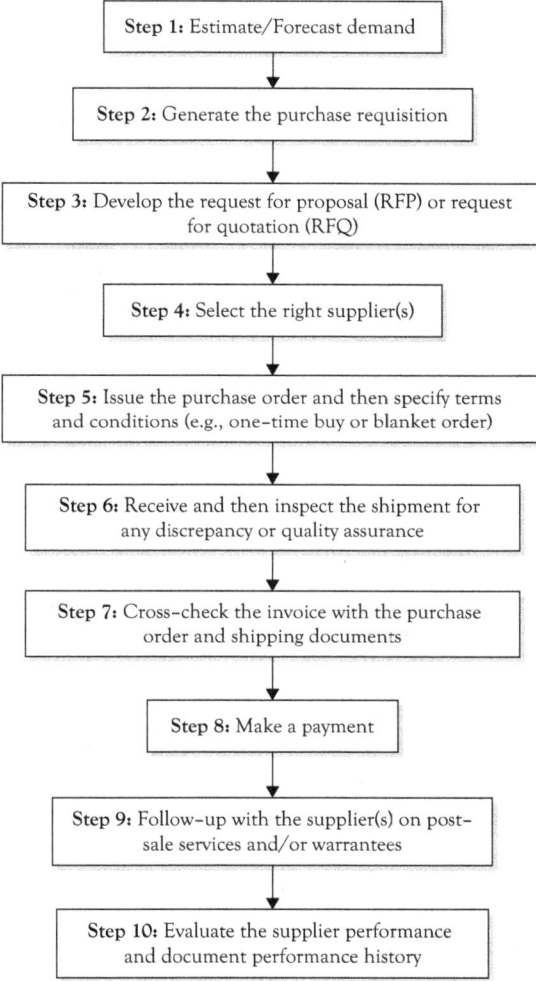

Figure 3.2 Medical asset purchasing procedures

3.4   Utilizing Third-party Logistics Service Providers (3PLs) for Healthcare Deliveries

A third-party logistics service provider (3PL) refers to a for-hire, independent service provider that performs all or part of logistics functions for the buyer, the seller, and the manufacturer of raw materials, parts or components, goods in process, or finished products without taking the title of those goods (Maltz and Ellram 2000; Zhou et al. 2008;

Perçin and Min 2013). The logistics functions performed by the 3PL can encompass a various spectrum of logistics activities such as transportation, warehousing, data access, logistics information system development, spare-parts distribution, inventory management, freight bill payment and audit, and value-added services including packaging, labeling, and return management (Sink and Langley 1997; Lieb and Miller 2002). Since the 3PL enables its user to focus on its core competency (e.g., quality medical care of the hospital and potent drug development of the pharmaceutical company), its use can help the healthcare provider improve its overall efficiency by better utilizing its given resources for what it can do best.

Recognizing the 3PL benefit potentials and popularity, a growing number of healthcare organizations have begun to exploit 3PL services. Though still limited, healthcare products currently represent about 5 percent of the total 3PL volume globally, and approximately 15 to 20 percent of such volume is associated with the logistics operations of pharmaceuticals (Burnson 2013). For example, both leading 3PLs and niche-oriented 3PLs stepped into the healthcare delivery market to manage the logistics operations of medical supplies and devices to healthcare providers. There are more than 140 3PLs in North America that are capable of managing healthcare logistics for their clients. Table 3.2 lists some niche-oriented 3PLs that focus on the healthcare or pharmaceutical logistics services.

3.5   Managing Pharmaceutical Supply Chains

As of 2011, the global pharmaceutical market was estimated to be worth US$880 billion a year with a growth rate of 5 to 7 percent and was expected to reach US$1.2 trillion by 2016 (IMS Health Incorporated 2012; International Federation of Pharmaceutical Manufacturers and Associations 2013). The 10 largest drug manufacturers control over one-third of this market, several with sales of more than US$10 billion a year and profit margins of about 30 percent (World Health Organization 2014a). Six of them (e.g., Johnson & Johnson, Pfizer, and GlaxoSmithKline) are based in the United States and four (e.g., Roche and Norvatis) in Europe. It is predicted that North and South America, Europe, and Japan would continue to account for a majority (85 percent) of the global pharmaceutical markets well into the

Table 3.2 A selected list of 3PLs that provide healthcare logistics services

3PLs	Key specialty service areas in healthcare logistics
AirNet Systems	Expedited services for medical device pick-ups and deliveries via air
APL Logistics	Time-definite services and value-added services for healthcare products
Bender Group	Multiclient, dedicated warehousing for healthcare products
C.H. Robinson	Temperature-controlled logistics services for healthcare products with global technology solutions
Cardinal Health Integrated Logistics	Cold chain storage in temperature-controlled facilities, assistance with ensuring product integrity during storage and shipping
CaseStack	Full-scalable services of retail healthcare products including billing or claim management, SKU level monitoring, shipment tracking
DSC Logistics	Pharmaceutical distribution, information technology solutions, change management in the healthcare supply chain network
Genco	Closed-loop supply chain solutions (including return management) for pharmaceuticals, critical medical supplies, and medical devices
Hegele Logistics	Customized logistics and installation services of medical equipment such as MRI machines
Kenco Logistics	Cold storage and full-service transportation solutions for healthcare products
LeSaint Logistics	Inventory, transportation, and value-added service for pharmaceuticals
LifeScience Logistics	Customized distribution, quality assurance, regulatory support, and order-to-cash management of pharmaceuticals, biotech products, and medical devices
MD Logistics	Customized cold storage and global distribution of clinical specialty products and pharmaceuticals
Panalpina	End-to-end supply chain solutions including air freight services for healthcare products
Ruan	Bulk transportation, kitting, and subassembly of medical supplies
Syfan Logistics	Expedited delivery services for perishable healthcare products
Tucker Company Worldwide	High safety, expedited transportation of Rx and over-the-counter pharmaceuticals
Unyson Logistics	Transportation optimization and network analysis of pharmaceuticals
WSI	Integrated supply chain solutions including call center management and order processing of healthcare products

twenty-first century (The Association of the British Pharmaceutical Industry 2013; World Health Organization 2014b). In particular, as shown in Table 3.3, both China and Brazil representing two developing economies have emerged as the fastest growing pharmaceutical markets, while the European market has been tapering off. Also, the pharmaceutical demand for developing countries in both Asia and Africa is expected to grow at a faster rate than Europe due to explosive population growths in the recent past. This changing market pattern can cause serious imbalances between pharmaceutical demand and supply, unless a large volume of affordable drugs can be distributed to emerging economies in Asia, Africa (especially Sub-Saharan African countries), Central and South America from the United States, and European countries where a vast majority of drugs are developed and produced. Such imbalances can only be avoided with the design and establishment of more efficient pharmaceutical supply chains across the world. With that in mind, the following subsections will explain what it takes to build the more efficient, resilient, and safe pharmaceutical supply chain.

3.5.1 Understanding Drug Distribution Channels

The most obvious but formidable barrier to healthcare access arises from a serious shortage of essential drugs, since the patient's disease cannot be controlled and cured without them. Such a shortage is often caused by a logistics hurdle of distributing drugs from the point of manufacturing to the point of consumption. Although a geographical distance is mainly attributed to that hurdle, there are a host of other factors such as a lack of logistics infrastructure and proper mode of transportation in the drug consumer's country that can compound the logistical problem. To make matters worse, this logistics hurdle increases drug prices and then makes essential drugs less affordable. Examples of added logistics costs include: warehousing and storage cost, inventory cost, shipping cost, import tariff, local tax, port charges, value-added tax, middle-men's margin, and inspection cost. Such added costs can easily raise the drug price by more than 60 percent as illustrated by Table 3.4.

Table 3.3 The size of the global pharmaceutical market

Country	2016 (Projected)			2011			2009		
	Rank	Market size (in $ million)	Compound annual growth rate	Rank	Market size (in $ million)	Growth rate	Rank	Market size (in $ million)	Growth rate
United States	1	$350,000–380,000	1~4%	1	$322,290	3%	1	$301,095	6%
Japan	3	105,000–135,000	0~3%	2	111,642	16%	2	89,865	17%
China	2	155,000–165,000	15~18%	3	66,805	22%	3	45,261	24%
Germany	5	39,000–49,000	0~3%	4	44,916	7%	4	41,287	2%
France	6	32,000–42,000	–2~1%	5	41,197	6%	5	40,452	5%
Brazil	4	42,000–52,000	12~15%	6	28,465	23%	10	17,629	8%
Italy	7	23,000–33,000	0~03%	7	28,357	7%	6	27,085	1%
Spain		No longer ranked in the top 10		8	22,679	2%	7	22,722	1%
Canada	8	19,000–29,000	0~3%	9	22,294	3%	9	19,143	0%
United Kingdom		No longer ranked in the top 10		10	21,564	6%	8	19,830	–11%

Source: The Association of the British Pharmaceutical Industry (2012); IMS Health Report (2012). *Global Pharmaceutical Industry and Market,* http://www.abpi.org.uk/industry-info/knowledge-hub/global-industry/Pages/industry-market-.aspx#fig1, retrieved on February, 17, 2014; IMS Health Report (2012), *The Global Use of Medicines: Outlook Through 2016,* Parsippany, NJ: IMS Institute.

Table 3.4 *An illustrated list of added logistics costs for pharmaceuticals*

	Armenia	Brazil	Kenya	Mauritius	Nepal	Tanzania	South Africa	Sri Lanka	Average
Import tariff		11.7%		5%	4%	10%			
Port charges			8%			1%		4%	
Clearance and freight			1%	5%	1.5%	2%			
Pre-shipment inspection			2.75%			1.2%			
Pharmacy board fee						2%			
Importer's margin					10%			25%	
Value-added-tax	20%	18%					14%		
State government tax		6%							
Wholesaler's margin	25%	7%	15%	14%	10%		21.2%	8.5%	
Retailer's margin	25%	22%	20%	27%	16%	50%	50%	16.3%	
Other hidden cost	17.5%	17.6%	7.45%	8.6%	6.5%	8.1%	0%	10.1%	
Total mark-up	87.5%	82.3%	54.2%	59.6%	48%	74.3%	85.2%	63.9%	68.6%

Source: Adapted and slightly modified from the Report of the International Federation of Pharmaceutical Manufacturers and Associations (2013).

To better understand how the drug distribution channel works, we should first figure out how drugs are made, distributed, and sold to the end-customers and who the main players are in the drug supply chain. Generally speaking, the drug supply chain involves multiple phases of business activities: primary manufacturing, secondary manufacturing, distribution, wholesaling, and retail sales as depicted in Figure 3.2. One thing to note in this supply chain is that although wholesalers play a dominant role in distributing drugs to retailers, on-line pharmacies and independent (entrepreneurial) pharmacies can bypass the whole-sale process to eliminate middle-men's margins. With frequent mergers and acquisitions among the specialty drug retailers and their increasing purchasing power, some large drug store chains (e.g., Walgreen) also could bypass the wholesalers for dispensing their pharmaceuticals to the end-customers. Also, it is noted that some wholesalers own their own independent pharmacies. For example, McKesson has the Health Mart that is regarded as an independent pharmacy, while AmerisourceBergen owns the Good Neighbor Pharmacy as its own independent pharmacy. As illustrated earlier, the links between drug wholesalers and retailers are more complex and situation-specific than was shown in Figure 3.3.

Not to mention logistics hurdles, a drug shortage can be caused by poor demand planning. For example, statin drugs are known to be very effective in reducing plaque buildup in blood vessels and thus preventing a heart attack and stroke for people over 60 who previously suffered from such illness (Topol 2004). Under the new guidelines from the American Heart Association and the American College of Cardiology, statin users are expected to increase from 43.2 million Americans to 56 million. Especially, among senior citizens aged 60 to 75, 87 percent of men (up from 30 percent as of 2014) and 53 percent of women (up from 21 percent as of 2014) should take statins if they have not been using it (Weintraub 2014). Considering the fast growth of senior populations across the world and changes in people's diets consuming cholesterol-rich foods, its demand will far exceed the current projection. Ill-prepared demand planning and the subsequent production shortage of life-saving drugs such as statins can spell disaster. Similar shortages for other life-saving drugs such as chemotherapy drugs were reported. As such, healthcare providers should move away from the conventional strategy of passively

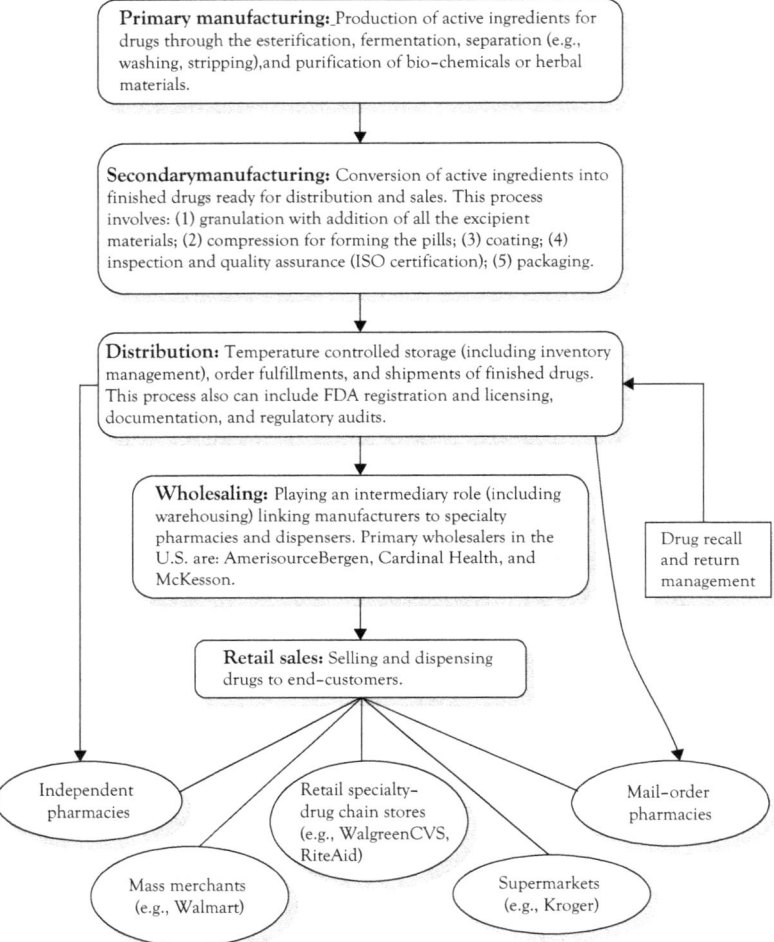

Figure 3.3 The prototypical pharmaceutical supply chain processes

reacting to demand fluctuations to the newer supply chain strategy of actively planning the demand well in advance. Also, from a supply chain standpoint, healthcare providers should consider sharing scarce life-saving drugs among them by cross-hauling from one provider with a surplus to another one with a shortage. Furthermore, sharing the information regarding the real-time inventory status of life-saving drugs among partnering healthcare organizations will help remedy the temporary drug shortage problem.

3.5.2 Weeding Out Fake, Illicit, and Substandard Drugs from Their Distribution Channels

According to the National Crime Prevention Council (2014), as much as 10 percent of all pharmaceuticals in the global supply chain might be counterfeits and in some developing countries they might account for as high as 70 percent of all drug trades. The proliferation of counterfeited drugs not only leads to huge financial losses for the pharmaceutical industry, but also raises serious health concerns (ten Ham 2003). Although the problem of counterfeit drugs was usually confined to developing nations in Africa and Asia, it has been rapidly spreading to other parts of the world including developed countries such as the United States. For example, tainted steroids caused the nationwide fungal meningitis outbreak in the United States and killed 64 people and sickened another 687 in 2012 (The Associated Press 2013). Similarly, in 2008, the contaminated blood thinner called carbohydrate Heparin imported from China killed 81 Americans even after it passed through several layers of screening procedures (Greenemeir 2008). Thus, the problem of counterfeit or substandard drugs has become a top concern among consumers, government health officials (especially drug regulatory agencies), pharmaceutical manufacturers, and healthcare providers.

A counterfeit (fake) drug is a medication or pharmaceutical product that is produced and sold with the intent to deceptively represent its origin, identity, authenticity, or potency (Davison 2011). Counterfeiting can apply to both branded and generic products and a counterfeit drug may contain insufficient (inappropriate quantities of) active ingredients, or none, may be improperly processed within the body (e.g., absorption by the body), may contain ingredients that are not on the label (which may be harmful or genuine), or may be supplied with inaccurate or fake packaging and labeling (World Health Organization 2014a). There are various ways to combat the proliferation of counterfeit drugs. One of those ways includes the identification of a weak link of the pharmaceutical supply chain where counterfeit drugs can sneak into. Such identification necessitates a clear understanding of the physical flows of those drugs throughout the supply chain. To figure out how and where those drugs can sneak into the pharmaceutical supply chain, we can draw the detailed supply chain map of drugs vulnerable to counterfeiting. Figure 3.3 illustrates the supply chain map of anti-malarial drugs and then points out the weak links of its supply chain where counterfeits can infiltrate. Figures 3.4 shows some illegal distribution channels or routes (displayed in red dotted lines) that can be exploited to disseminate counterfeit drugs by street vendors and unlicensed dispensers. Due to the irregularity and the illicit elements (e.g., a gray distribution channel and unregulated street vendors) of the aforementioned supply chain activities, the SC map for anti-malarial drugs shown in Figure 3.4 looks different from the map for a prototypical pharmaceutical supply chain shown in Figure 3.3. To cut off the supplies of

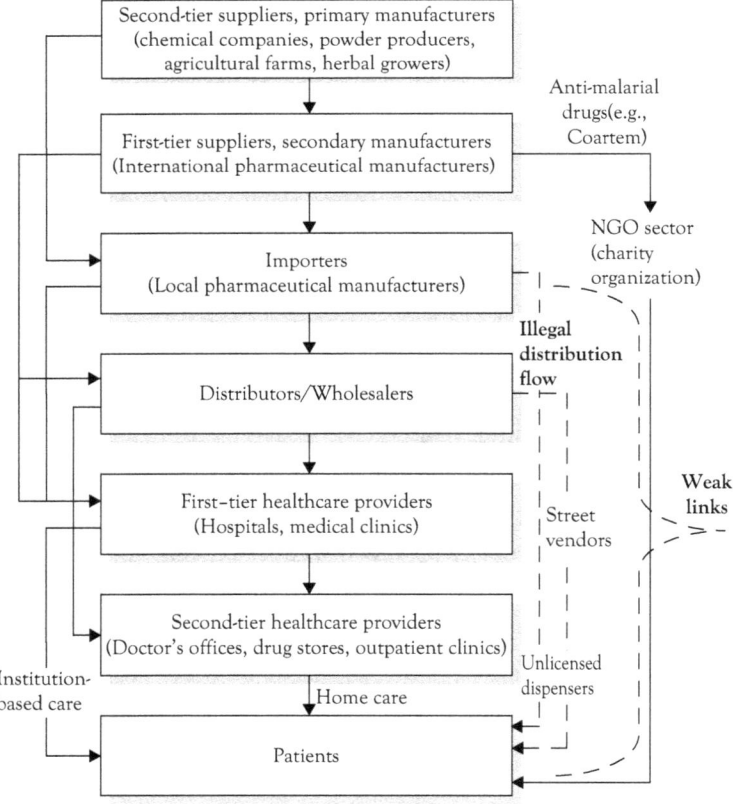

Figure 3.4 The supply chain map of anti-malarial drugs in Africa

Source: Adapted and slightly modified from Min (2012).

counterfeit drugs, local government health officials should better monitor and regulate street vendors who become primary sources of anti-malarial drugs in Africa while blocking potential smuggling routes. Some of these fake or substandard anti-malarial drugs are frequently sold by the street vendors alongside blue jeans, shoes, and wheelbarrows. The popularity of street vendors has something to do with their convenient access, because they can travel anywhere (including remote villages) and never require prescriptions for drug purchases. Part of the reasons why many consumers buy anti-malarial drugs from the street vendors is a lack of logistics infrastructure and established distribution channel that hinders the access of licit medicines from government medical clinics or charity organizations that often give licit anti-malarial drugs away for free. As such, Min (2012) proposed piggybacking on the pre-established distribution channel of daily necessities such as popular soft-drinks, while establishing the local satellite drug distribution facilities that were in close proximity to isolated villages and could store an extra amount of safety stocks sufficient enough for potential malaria outbreaks. Also, the local government policy has to be amended to stem the tide of counterfeit trades. A change in policy may include: increased "spot-check" inspection of medicines sold by the street vendors and increased enforcement of anti-counterfeit rules. However, simple policy changes and improved distribution practices alone cannot improve drug safety. Thus, the next subsection will discuss ways to leverage technology to strengthen the drug supply chain.

3.5.3   Maintaining Drug Supply Chain Security and Integrity

Considering the seriousness of counterfeiting to drug safety, numerous efforts were made in the recent past to make the drug supply chain more resilient from tempering or the infiltration of counterfeits. These efforts involve the constant tracking of drug flows throughout the supply chain and authentication of distributed drugs by using state-of-art technologies. One such technology includes radio frequency identification (RFID). RFID generally refers to a wireless device that carries data in transponders (i.e., tags) attached permanently to the asset (e.g., container, case, and pallet) and reads data stored on a microchip using radio waves (Carr et al. 2010; Min and Shin 2012). Data stored in the RFID tag can provide unique identification for manufactured items, goods in transit, physical locations, vehicle identities, and humans (The Association of the Automatic Identification and Data Capture Industry 2002).

With its ability to identify, track, and trace items automatically, RFID makes it easier to ensure that distributed drugs are authentic, free of tempering. Also, it creates an *electronic pedigree*—a record of the chain of custody from the point of production to the point of dispensing. An electronic pedigree improves patient safety and protects the public health by allowing wholesalers and retailers to rapidly identify, quarantine, and report suspected counterfeit drugs and conduct efficient, targeted product recalls (U.S. Food and Drug Administration 2005). For example, GlaxoSmithKline used RFID to improve the visibility of pharmaceutical products in the supply chain, and to curb drugs deemed susceptible to counterfeiting and theft (Bacheldor 2007). Pfizer placed RFID tags on the packages of certain highly counterfeited drugs such as Viagra (sildenafil), Lipitor, and Norvasc, and Zoloft to track those drugs from the manufacturer to the pharmacy by verifying the unique electronic product code (EPC) on the product packages (O'Connor 2006). Similarly, Purdue Pharma implemented large-scale item-level tagging by placing RFID tags on bottles of the pain reliever OxyContin (oxycodone) and Palladone (hydromorphone) to authenticate, track, and trace those medications susceptible to abuse, counterfeiting, and theft (Ramsey 2009). Despite a growing use and popularity of RFID in the pharmaceutical supply chain, RFID use is still limited due to its cost of tagging and various implementation hurdles illustrated in Figure 3.5 (Min and Shin 2012; Yao et al. 2012). As a cheaper alternative, bar coding is frequently used in the pharmaceutical industry to track and trace drugs with unit-dose identifiers that can document the drug's source, date of manufacture, lot number, and expiration dates.

Table 3.5 summarizes differences between bar coding and RFID systems. Although RFID has many advantages over bar coding, it is still far more expensive than bar coding and poses more challenges than bar coding for successful implementation. Thus, a choice between these two alternative systems will be up to each healthcare organization's financial resources, IT infrastructure, and readiness.

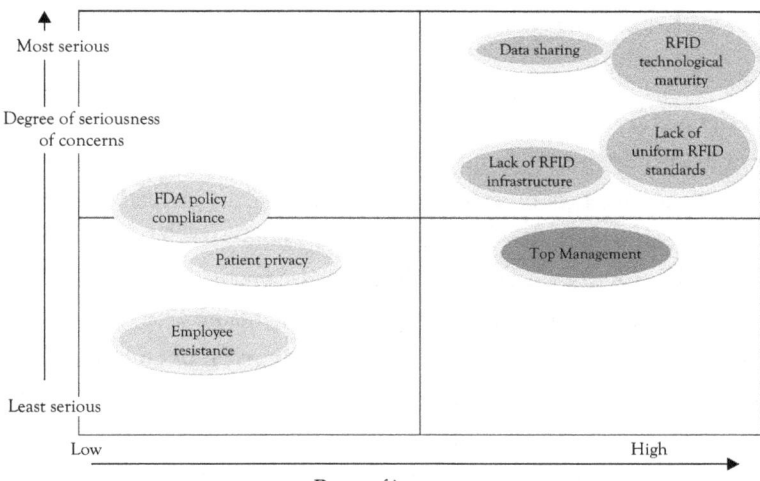

Figure 3.5 RFID implementation hurdles

Table 3.5 A comparison of bar coding to RFID

Bar coding	RFID
Data transmission through standard marking with vertical bars	Data transmission through an RFID tag (both "active"- battery powered or "passive"- powered by the polling reader)
Obtain information by scanning data on a laser or charge-coupled device	Obtain information from the electronic product code (EPC) contained in tags through a reader and antenna (*wireless*)
One-dimensional information density	Multiple dimensional information density—an ability to encode more information than one-dimensional bar code
Less expensive	More expensive (i.e., 10 to 50 times more expensive than one-dimensional bar code)
A single identifier (*read one bar code at a time*)	Multiple identifiers (*read multiple tags within its transmission field*)—faster reading
Read data (one at a time)	Read and write data (even unusual or harsh environments such as oily and dirty surfaces)
Short distance reading	Long distance reading (up to 6 to 10 feet): *higher frequency tags typically have longer read distances and faster data transfer rates than lower frequent tags*

3.5.4 Enhancing the Affordability of Drugs

While more potent drugs have been introduced to the world thanks to continuous investment in the research and development (R&D) of drugs, drug prices have risen continuously for the last few decades. This rapid rise in drug prices is of serious concern among the general public and healthcare providers alike since many (both non-essential and essential) drugs will be out of reach for needy patients. Some studies such as Atella et al. (2005) demonstrated that co-payments on medication (i.e., patient's out-of-pocket cost burden) reduced the consumption of both non-essential and essential drugs, and that the latter worsened the quality of healthcare. In particular, developing countries where most people must pay for their medicine out of their own pockets due to limited government aids for healthcare, rising drug prices will have serious consequences for public health. For example, in Malaysia one month's supply of ranitidine (a drug for stomach ulcers) was equivalent to approximately three days' wages for a typical government worker, and one month's supply of fluoxetine (an antidepressant) would cost around 26 days' wages and subsequently made these drugs unaffordable for many needy individuals. As such, dramatic measures including some forms of price regulation are needed to ease the burden of the high cost of drugs. Prior to developing these measures, we need to examine what typically comprises drug prices and what may have caused hikes in drug prices. The detailed components of typical drug price are recapitulated in Table 3.6. Table 3.6 shows a host of factors that can influence the particular drug price. Especially, if drugs are imported from other countries, those drugs will become far more expensive than the domestically produced drugs. That is to say, one way to control skyrocketing drug prices is to increase domestic or local production and distribution of drugs.

In particular, prices of brand-name prescription drugs in the United States are much higher than in Canada, the United Kingdom, and other countries in the Organization for Economic Cooperation and Development (OECD) (Kanavos et al. 2013). For example, Nasonex (used for allergies) was $105 in the United States and only $29 in Canada. As such, in 2012 the American spent an average of $892 on prescription drugs, while the Canadian spent only $420 on the

Table 3.6 Drug price components

Stages of the drug supply chain	Components
Stage 1: Manufacturer's Selling Price (MSP)	Cost of research and development (R&D) Cost of manufacturing including cost of acquiring active ingredients Cost of order fulfillments Manufacturer's profit margin Insurance and freight
Stage 2: Total Landed Price	Port and inspection charges Customs clearance cost Import duties (customs duties) Foreign currency exchange loss Importer's mark-up or commission Pharmacy board fee or national drug authority fee Banking fee Import license fee (if necessary) Local transportation and distribution cost Relationship cost (e.g., grease payment) if necessary Other miscellaneous fees (e.g., defense levy in Sri Lanka, consular invoice fee in Central America)
Stage 3: Wholesale Price	Cost of warehousing and inventory Mark-up by the wholesaler Regional or state tax
Stage 4: Retail Price	Mark-up by the retailer Local tax Advertising cost
Stage 5: Dispense Price	Dispensing fees Value added tax (VAT) or Goods & Service Tax (GST)

Note: Manufacturer's discounts or rebates are excluded from this list.

average, and the European in EU countries spent, on an average, $375 (IMS Institute for Healthcare Informatics 2012). Although drug price differentials between different countries are not uncommon, a significant price differential for brand-name drugs between the United States and Canada has led many Americans to purchase branded prescription drugs illegally from Canadian pharmacies. Although comparatively inexpensive drugs available across the border help Americans relieve the burden of their healthcare costs, this drug re-importation practice is illegal and may cause medicine shortages in Canada. Similarly, differences in drug prices between nations could lead to the illegal parallel trade of branded drugs. For instance, some wholesalers bought drugs at state-regulated prices in countries such as Spain or Greece and then sold them back to the U.K. market where drugs were more expensive. One sensible way to deal with this dilemma is to make more generic drugs available to U.S. patients, when the patents of the unprecedented number of branded drugs will expire within the next few years. Unlike some branded drugs that are subject to distribution restrictions, generic drugs are free of such restrictions and can bypass wholesalers, thereby making generic drugs more accessible and affordable to the needy patients. Generic drugs constitute as much as an 80 percent savings in drug cost, as compared to branded drugs. The use of generic prescription drugs has saved the U.S. healthcare system $217 billion in 2012 alone and $1.3 trillion over the last decade (Generic Pharmaceutical Association 2013).

Another way to control rising drug prices is to maintain a sufficient amount of older but still potent drugs (e.g., pre-existing drugs for hypertension), which are usually cheaper than new alternative drugs. In fact, about 70 percent of the annual cost increase in drug purchases is due to the high price of new medicines introduced to the market less than 5 years ago (Dukes et al. 2003). However, a great majority of new drugs tend to be nothing but unexciting alternatives to older drugs. In addition to the preceding schemes, the increased exploitation of collaborative purchasing for drug price concession seems to make sense. For example, Georgia's Department of Community Health (DCH) used a single Pharmacy Benefits Manager (PBM) to negotiate drug manufacturers' rebates and discounts to control the costs of prescription drugs for Medicare patients. Similarly, multiple states such as Delaware, Missouri, New Mexico, Ohio, and West Virginia formed the RxIS Coalition to negotiate the manufacturer's discounts for prescribed drugs for their state employees' health plans (Altarum Institute 2011).

3.5.5 Drug Pricing Strategy

As discussed earlier, the way drug prices are set is quite different from the way ordinary product prices are determined in the business world, since the former is influenced by many different stakeholders (e.g., patient, physician, insurer, pharmacy, and government regulatory agency) and the different structure of market competition (e.g., single source branded drugs versus generic drugs). As such, in a pharmaceutical market, *reference pricing* is the norm. Reference pricing refers to a pricing mechanism where a buying agent such as the insurer determines a reimbursement price and then the user or patient or insurer pays the difference if the chosen medicine is more expensive than the pre-set reimbursement price (López-Casasnovas and Puig-Junoy 2000). Reflecting the reference pricing mechanism, patients typically decide on the over-the-counter (OTC) drug purchase and pays for it. However, as far as prescription drugs are concerned, its pricing can vary because an ultimate payor can change from one type of prescription drugs to another (van der Meer and Kerkhofs 2008). For instance, if the prescription drug cannot be reimbursed, the patient pays for the chosen drug and then absorbs the cost. On the other hand, if the prescription drug can be reimbursed, the multiple parties involving the insurer, the government, and the patient pay for the chosen drug, while its ultimate cost will be shared by the patient, his or her employer, and the government. That is to say, if the patient covers all the drug purchase expenditures, he or she will be more sensitive to pricing. On the other hand, if the drug purchase can be mostly reimbursed, the patient will be less sensitive to pricing.

Generally, drug pricing should factor into a multitude of variables: (1) proven potency (or effectiveness) including the percentage of patients whose pains or diseases can be relieved or how soon the patient can experience the drug's positive effect; (2) the risk of side effects; (3) the reimbursement or co-payment status (e.g., full or majority reimbursement for life-saving drugs); (4) the level of competition in the market (e.g., single-source versus generic competition, and first-mover versus follow-the-leader); (5) the newness of the drug; and (6) government price control or regulations. Some of the pricing schemes that can be used in the pharmaceutical industry are as follows:

1. *Volume-based pricing* is widely used and takes the form of incremental quantity discounts, customer loyalty programs, year-end customer bonuses, and other similar schemes. It is often used to decrease price

transparency as well as increase the cost of switching to alternative drugs for customers (van der Meer and Kerkhofs 2008).

2. *Bundled pricing* is a pricing scheme where two complementary products or services are priced together in a bundle, which makes it difficult for the customer to figure out the true price for each and thus make price comparison to alternative medicines less transparent. Bundling may be used to push and support one drug, using the market success and notoriety of another drug it is bundled with and thus increasing overall profit for both products (van der Meer and Kerkhofs 2008). For example, Sandoz Pharmaceuticals once bundled Clozaril or Clozapil, which was effective in treating schizophrenia, with the compulsory blood monitoring system handling the side effect. However, bundled pricing is vulnerable to antitrust lawsuits (Hurwitz 1991).

3. *Dynamic pricing* is a relatively new pricing scheme that changes prices constantly over time (even minute by minute) with the intent of testing the water on a real-time basis. With the emergence of online pharmacies, this pricing scheme may be useful for attracting patients who seek bargains for over-the-counter or generic drugs.

3.6   Handling Medical Waste

One of the byproducts of healthcare services is medical waste. Medical waste consists of a broad range of materials including solids, liquids, sharps, blood, chemicals, and body parts that are considered potentially hazardous, infectious, toxic, or radioactive. Based on the various sources of medical waste categorized by the World Health Organization (2011), Table 3.7 illustrates many different types of medical waste. Among these various types of medical waste, infectious and pathological wastes represent a majority of the hazardous waste, up to 15 percent of the total medical waste from healthcare activities. Sharps represent about 1 percent of the total medical waste, but they are a major source of disease transmission if not properly managed. Chemicals and pharmaceuticals account for about 3 percent of the total medical waste, while genotoxic, radioactive, and heavy metal content account for around 1 percent of the total medical waste (World Health Organization 2011). Since medical waste poses a high risk of contamination and pollution regardless of its type, it has to be

Table 3.7 **A list of medical waste**

Type	Example
Infectious waste	Waste contaminated with blood and its by-products, cultures and stocks of infectious agents, waste from patients in isolation wards, discarded diagnostic samples or gauzes containing blood and body fluids, infected animals from laboratories, and contaminated materials (swabs, bandages) and equipment (such as disposable medical devices)
Pathological waste	Recognizable human tissues and body parts, animal or human feces, contaminated animal carcasses, and blood-borne pathogens
Sharps	Syringes, needles, surgical scissors, disposable scalpels, and blades
Chemicals	Solvents and disinfectants neutralizing microbes
Pharmaceuticals	Expired, unused, and contaminated drugs, vaccines, and sera
Genotoxic waste	Highly hazardous, mutagenic, teratogenic, or carcinogenic (e.g., chemotherapy, cytotoxic drugs used in cancer treatment and their metabolites)
Radioactive waste	Glassware contaminated with radioactive diagnostic material or radio-therapeutic materials
Heavy metal waste	Waste that exhibits metallic properties such as mercury, plutonium, and lead (e.g., broken mercury thermometers, blood pressure cuffs, and cantor tubes)

segregated from the point of its source and then properly managed until its safe disposal. Unlike the ordinary solid waste, medical waste typically requires specific disposal and handling procedures tailored for each waste due to its varying nature and regulatory stipulations (Hassan et al. 2008). For example, used syringes or broken thermometers are typically disposed in containers at the medical facility to prevent contamination of healthcare workers and others (e.g., hospital patients) who can be exposed to those. In addition, these containers become part of the medical waste supply chain as they are retained for eventual disposal at either incineration or dumping sites. Prior to dumping, medical waste usually goes through advanced decontamination processes using microwave and autoclave technologies. Only after such treatments, medical waste is allowed for disposal in landfills (Al-Shallash and Shereif 2007). Considering this inherent complexity associated with medical waste treatment and disposal, the next subsections will elaborate on the environmental implications of medical waste management and green supply chain strategy relevant to medical waste treatment and disposal.

3.6.1   Understanding the Environmental Implications of Medical Waste

Medical waste contributes to a wide range of environmental degradation throughout its life cycle and entire supply chain. As shown in Figure 3.6, medical waste originates from healthcare activities performed by hospitals, medical clinics, medical laboratories, pharmacies, mortuaries, blood banks, nursing homes, and other healthcare facilities. Depending on its nature and type, this waste will be separated from general solid waste and then disposed at the nearby landfill, discharged to sewage systems, or sent to the incinerator. If not properly managed, the disposed medical waste can be a major source of pollution and contamination. For example, formaldehyde and solvents used for pathology can be diluted and flushed down to sanitary sewer, which then eventually pollutes drinking water. Also, highly toxic chemotherapy and antineoplastic chemicals that are incinerated can emit pollutants into the air and then deplete stratospheric ozone that contributes to climate changes. In particular, the incineration of heavy metal waste containing lead, mercury, and cadmium can create serious adverse health effects by generating dioxins and furans. To reduce these adverse health effects of medical waste, more systematic waste treatment and disposal procedures should be developed. Such procedures may start with the life cycle assessment of medical waste.

Life cycle assessment (LCA) is a popular tool used to develop waste management strategies. The main goal of LCA is to compare the environmental performance of healthcare products and services throughout their life cycles, while enabling healthcare providers to choose the waste management option that provides the maximum protection of natural environments in an economically feasible and socially acceptable manner. LCA also aims to improve the overall environmental performance and public image of a healthcare organization. LCA covers the entire life cycle of medical waste encompassing waste generation, sorting and separation, treatment, storage, transfer and transportation, reuse, recycling, and ultimate disposal. LCA is also helpful for identifying specific areas of healthcare supply chain processes where environmental improvements can be made. LCA is typically comprised of three interrelated components: a life cycle inventory analysis, a life cycle impact analysis, and a life cycle

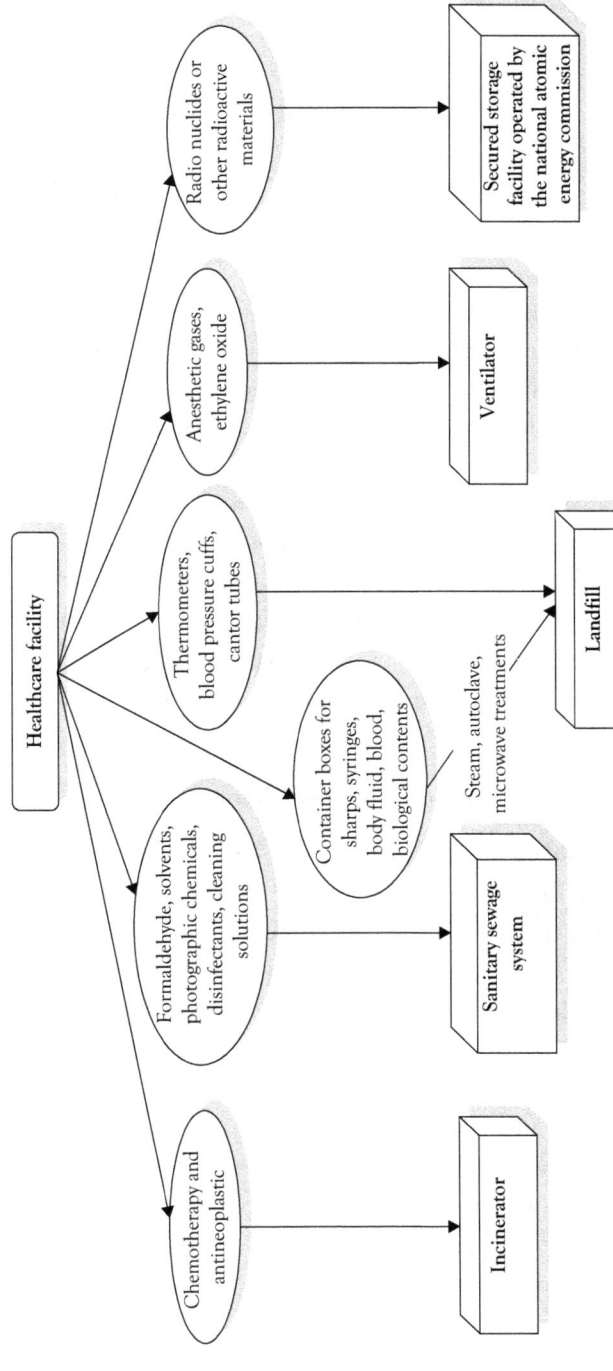

Figure 3.6 A disposal process map of the hazardous medical waste

improvement analysis. The details of these components are described as follows (Svoboda 1995):

1. *Life Cycle Inventory.* An objective, data-based process of quantifying ecological footprints including the extent of air pollutants, water-borne effluents, solid waste, and other environmental releases incurred throughout the life cycle of a healthcare product, process, or activity.

2. *Life Cycle Impact Assessment.* An evaluative process of assessing the effects of the environmental findings identified in the inventory component. The impact assessment should address both ecological and human health impacts, as well as social, cultural, and economic impacts.

3. *Life Cycle Improvement Analysis.* An analysis of opportunities to reduce or mitigate the environmental impact throughout the whole life cycle of a healthcare product, process, or activity. This analysis may include both quantitative and qualitative measures of improvement, such as changes in product design, raw material usage, industrial processes (e.g., purchases), consumer use, and waste disposal.

3.6.2 *"Greening" the Healthcare Supply Chain*

In the previous subsection, we discussed about the potential environmental risks of dumping, evaporating, draining, and incinerating medical waste. Regardless of waste disposal methods, it would still be difficult to remove infectious microbes or harmful biochemical substances entirely from medical waste. Therefore, the best way to control medical waste is to reduce its sources in the first place. Source reduction strategy may include: (1) *substitutable product development* by using more environmental-friendly ingredients for new healthcare products; (2) *environmentally preferable purchasing (or green purchasing)* by prioritizing environmentally conscious suppliers (e.g., suppliers complying with environmental laws, regulations, and standards) over others or avoiding excessive purchases that build up unnecessary inventories and subsequent waste (e.g., expired drugs and obsolete medical supplies); (3) *resource recovery* by reusing and recycling second-hand medical equipment, supplies, and devices; (4) *medical process* change by revolutionizing the traditional medical procedure (e.g., anesthesia and cancer treatment) that heavily relied on chemical and radioactive treatments.

To elaborate, a substitutable product refers to the product that can meet the same needs of customers with the same functionality and the comparable price and thus can be used to replace another existing product. For example, a conventional thermometer frequently used in the medical facility contains highly toxic mercury whose exposure can cause serious health problems such as tremors, impaired vision and hearing, paralysis, insomnia, kidney failures, and breakdown in nervous, digestive, respiratory, and immune systems. Concerned with these potential health hazards, a medical device manufacturer has recently introduced a non-mercury thermometer that used non-toxic isoamyl benzoate and dye and thus could eliminate the risk of mercury poisoning resulting from the broken thermometer.

Put simply, environmentally preferable purchasing (EPP) is the practice of purchasing goods and services that cause less harm to humans and the environment than competing goods and services that serve the same purpose (Simcich 2014). EPP is a proactive (or preventive) measure for source reduction that reduces adverse environmental or health effects related to healthcare products or service before they occur. Its main goals are as follows (Practice Greenhealth 2014):

- To reduce or eliminate medical waste disposal and the need for healthcare worker safety measures
- To provide a healthier environment for patients and healthcare workers through reduced exposure to hazardous substances such as disinfectants, solvents, and pathogens
- To create opportunities for positive publicity and promotion of the healthcare organization

For example, Fairview Health Services replaced polystyrene coolers that were bulky and difficult to recycle with a compostable and biodegradable cooler made from cornstarch to ship temperature-sensitive medicines to their patients. By changing their purchasing practice in a more environmental friendly manner, they were able to eliminate waste stream from their healthcare supply chain (Waters 2014).

Resource recovery refers to the extraction and reclamation of valuable resources and energy from the waste stream for a next use through reusing, recycling, composting, or energy generation. Its main goals are to reduce the amount of waste generated from healthcare activities, minimize the consumption of virgin natural resources, and create value (e.g., fertilizer from the composted organic materials) out of discarded but useful materials. For example, Kaiser Permanente began to use recyclable sterile wraps for the protection of surgical instruments instead of single use, disposable sterile wraps and was able to reduce the source of medical waste in the operating room while saving waste disposal costs by more than $94,000 per year (Kaiser Permanente 2010). Figure 3.7 shows the process of recovering valuable resources and energy from medical waste.

Another innovative way to reduce the waste source is to change conventional medical treatment processes, which necessitates less environmental-friendly materials or generates highly toxic materials. For example, the healthcare worker who is exposed to waste anesthesia

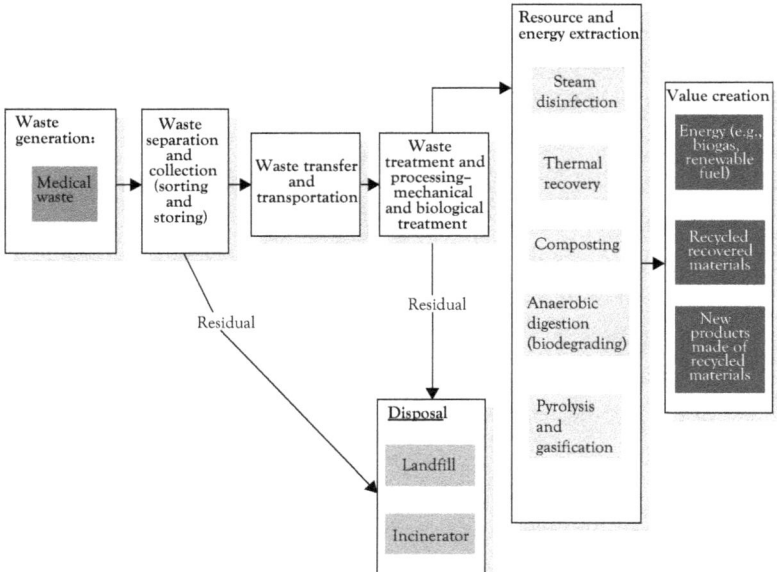

Figure 3.7 A resource recovery process of medical waste

gases can suffer from a variety of health problems such as dizziness, feelings of light headiness, nausea, fatigue, headache, irritability, and depression. To avoid such an exposure, some dentists and medical doctors consider using hypnosis or acupuncture for pain relief or surgical anesthesia. Thus, a wider use of this kind of alternative medical treatment can potentially help reduce harmful medical waste.

CHAPTER 4

Performance Metrics for the Healthcare Supply Chain

Once a healthcare organization embraces supply chain principles to innovate the management practices and then enhance the productivity, there may be a need to know how well the organization has been performing with respect to patient satisfaction and competitiveness. If the supply chain performances are lagging behind patient satisfaction standards and the performances of your peers, then it is important to know what causes such lagging performances and also find measures to continuously improve the supply chain performances. The healthcare organization's conceptual framework is depicted in Figure 4.1. In particular, defining performance measures is at the core of continuous improvement of healthcare productivity. Defining performance measures involve the development of a measuring yardstick that would be a basis for fair evaluation and the comparison of the healthcare organization's supply chain performances. To have more meaningful measures of the entire supply chain processes as opposed to each healthcare unit (a department or an organization), such a yardstick should have the following traits:

- *Multidimensional*: Since the supply chain spans many different boundaries of the business functions and organizations, its yardstick should cover more than one aspect of healthcare processes. For example, the healthcare organization's effort to reduce sourcing costs through high-volume purchasing results in excessive amount of supplies and obsolete inventories of medical supplies and pharmaceuticals.
- *Specific*: The supply chain performance measure generally reflects a big picture performance of cross-functional and cross-organizational integrated activities, but it should also

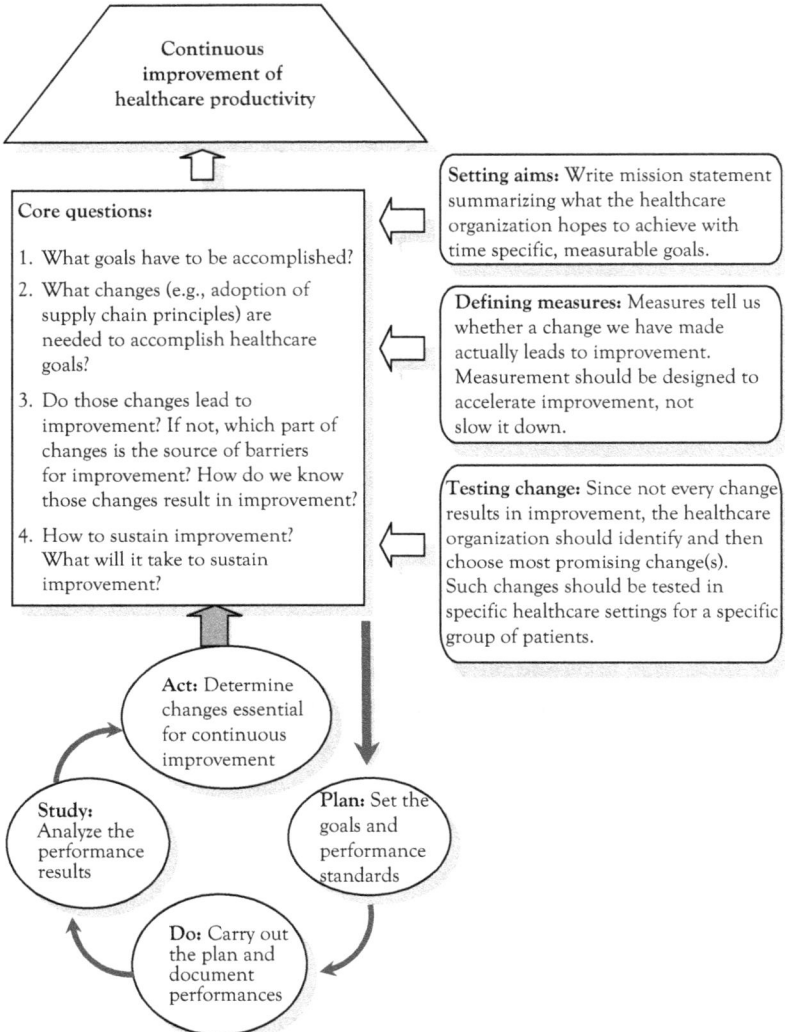

Figure 4.1 Action plans for the continuous improvement of healthcare productivity

Source: Adapted and modified from Primary Healthcare, Inc. (2003).

be specific enough to pinpoint exactly what a yardstick intends to measure. For example, a broadly defined traditional measure such as hospital bed utilization alone may not reflect the true healthcare productivity, if most hospital beds are

occupied by long-term care patients and thus are in short
supply for other patients who need urgent care.

- *Universal*: A performance measure that can only be used
  for any particular hospital or medical settings will not be
  appropriate for a meaningful supply chain performance
  metric. For example, the pharmaceutical price differs from
  one country to another and can thus influence the cost
  of healthcare. Thus, a simple comparison of healthcare
  performance with respect to the aggregate healthcare cost can
  be misleading.
- *Repeatable*: Since supply chain performance has to be
  monitored constantly over time, a one-time measure will not
  be appropriate for measuring the supply chain performance.
  For example, the number of healthcare workers or the amount
  of investment in the healthcare facility and technology at a
  certain point of time cannot be a proper supply chain performance metric.
- *Quantifiable*: Although some patient service measures such
  as the level of patient satisfaction are hard to quantify,
  ambiguous and subjective measures cannot provide a clear
  yardstick for evaluating the comparative performance of a
  particular healthcare practice and process against others. Thus,
  metrics that can be expressed in numerical terms (for example, percentage, ratio, time) are more useful for measuring the
  supply chain performance.
- *Traceable*: Performance measures that are based on
  confidential information (like patient medical history),
  proprietary information, or untraceable data may not be
  appropriate for measuring the supply chain performance.
  If the necessary performance data are hard to come by, metrics
  based on such data will be difficult to implement and thus
  will be less meaningful.

With the preceding discussion in mind, the next subsections will elaborate
on the performance metrics that can be useful for measuring healthcare
supply chain performances and the subsequent healthcare productivity.

4.1   Key Performance Indicators

Generally speaking, a key performance indicator (KPI) is a measure of how well an organization is making progress toward its strategic goals and how well it is performing against targets or expectations. KPI is used to show what kind of improvements are made over time and determine what constitutes critical success factors. Since the organization's goals and missions are different from each other, the KPI varies from one organization to another, one business function to another, and one industry to another. For example, the KPIs for a healthcare insurance company may include average cost per claim and claims ratio, whereas the KPIs for a hospital may include inpatient mortality rate, readmission rate, and occupancy rate. Regardless of these differences, the KPIs can be categorized into three types: (1) *process KPI*, which measures the efficiency of a healthcare delivery process such as bed turnover and a number of rings before a patient phone call is answered; (2) *input KPI*, which measures assets and resources invested in or used to render healthcare services such as dollars spent on medical equipment or budgets set aside for healthcare worker (e.g., nurse) training; and (3) *output KPI*, which measures the financial and nonfinancial results of business activities such as return-on-investment (ROI), total operating margin, days of cash on hand, and market share (Kaplan 2009). Also, KPIs can be targeted to measure performance that is relevant to *all service users* (for example, waiting time for hospital admission) or to measure aspects of healthcare services that are relevant to *specific service users* (for example, a percentage of children who are referred for speech therapy) (Health Information and Quality Authority 2013).

To understand and identify specific KPIs relevant to a particular healthcare organization, one should ask the following questions:

- What are your organization's strategic goals, mission statements, and value propositions?
- Which healthcare activities should be prioritized to maximize your patient's satisfaction?
- What are the best ways to communicate the progress of your organization's performance improvement efforts to your organization's patients and stakeholders?

- Is it possible to collect the required data?
- How can you visualize and simplify your performance improvement efforts?
- Are performance data or the evidences of performance improvements readily available to decision makers or stakeholders within an acceptable period of time?

For illustrative purposes, Table 4.1 summarizes the KPIs that can be employed by the hospital to monitor its performances (Infosys 2009).

Table 4.1 An illustrative list of hospital KPIs

Category	KPI	Examples of performance metrics	Main purposes
Clinical	*Hospital incidents*	• Number of patients acquiring infections • Frequency of transfusion reactions • Bed sores • Postoperative respiratory failures • Postoperative pulmonary embolism or deep vein thrombosis • Postoperative sepsis • Postoperative hip fracture • Postoperative hemorrhage or hematoma	Provide a quick snapshot on how the hospital is performing with regard to the quality of care. The drill down information provides insights on factors that need immediate corrective action.
	Mortality	• Postoperative or procedural death rate • Estimates of deaths from any cause within 30 days of a hospital admission	Useful for benchmarking the performance of the hospital and see how it has performed against national and state norms and against its peers
	Patient satisfaction	• Courtesy score for medical staff • Quality of meals, physician care, nursing care, and housekeeping services • Admission process score • Emergency response time	Provide valuable insights into making adjustments in areas such as efficiency of the admissions process and managing admission of patients to a clinical unit. It is also valuable for staff training, morale enhancement, and creative marketing.

(Continued)

Table 4.1 An illustrative list of hospital KPIs (Continued)

Category	KPI	Examples of performance metrics	Main purposes
		• Patient complaint handling • Percentage of patients who recommend the hospital to their friends and family	
Opera-tional	*Medical error*	• Wrong medication • Wrong diagnosis • Wrong dosage • Poor communication with the patient • Poor medication labeling or packaging • Overtesting • Overtreatments	Examine which options should be deployed to reduce preventable medical error. These options may include the use of technology such as computerized physician order entry (CPOE) and clinical decision support systems (CDSS) for allergy prompts, wireless patient identification, and sensors.
	Patient waiting time	• Waiting time for admission, discharge, triage, ambulance, and diagnosis (lab test and radiology)	Patient waiting time directly influences the patient satisfaction level. Such insight allows the hospital to identify improvement areas with longer waiting times.
	Average length of stay	• Admission rate (last day/ month to date/year to date) • Discharge rate (last day/ month to date/year to date)	Provide insights into the patient throughput for a hospital. Other things being equal, a shorter stay reduces the cost per discharge and shift care from inpatient to less expensive postacute settings. However, shorter stays tend to be more service intensive but more costly per day. Very short stays can also cause adverse health effects (e.g., less comfort and limited time for a full recovery of the patient).

Table 4.1 (Contiuned)

	Asset utilization rate	• Bed utilization rate • Medical equipment utilization time, maintenance time, and idle time	Assets generate revenue only when they are put to use. Tracking the performance of all hospital assets can have a huge impact on patient satisfaction and the bottom line. Low utilization levels lead to lost revenue and a very high utilization level leads to increased wait times, cancellations, and diversions.
Financial	*Payer performance*	• Percentage of claims paid • Reimbursements amount	Provide insights into how well payer's contracts are performing and which one needs renegotiation.
	Physician performance	• Revenue per physician • Reimbursements per physician	Provide insights into how each physician is performing in terms of number of cases, revenue per case, utilization cost per case, and bonuses and penalties incurred per physician.
	Hospital performance	• Revenue • Profit margin • Clinical cost reimbursement • Account receivable (AR) aging days	Provide a real-time snap shot of the hospital performance in terms of revenue, profit, margin, reimbursement versus utilization cost, AR by aging days and potential high risk, and AR that need immediate intervention.
	Emergency care expenses	• Ambulance diversion hours • Physician nonavailability	Ambulance diversions have a very high impact on the clinical outcome and are a direct revenue loss to the hospital. Efforts should be made to keep this to minimum levels.

(Continued)

Table 4.1 An illustrative list of hospital KPIs (Contiuned)

Category	KPI	Examples of performance metrics	Main purposes
	Added hospital expenses	• Overtime hours • Cost of rework and opportunity cost resulting from test errors • Legal costs associated with malpractice lawsuits	Provide an insight into capacity planning issues and have a direct impact on the bottom line as well as employee satisfaction. Test result errors result in lost revenue and resources, undermining the bottom line. Root cause analysis needs to be carried out to reduce these occurrences.

4.2 Healthcare Supply Chain Performance Metrics

In the previous section, we discussed about KPIs that can be used for a particular healthcare organization (namely, hospital) and setting. However, given that healthcare supply chain processes involve a number of partners and stakeholders, we need to assess not only performances of each functional unit, but also those of its supply chain partners. Thus, KPIs intended for each separate organization (or function) are not sufficient for evaluating the overall improvement of the entire supply chain (Bolstroff and Rosenbaum 2003). Considering this shortcoming of KPIs, we would like to introduce the supply chain performance metrics more relevant to measuring cross-functional healthcare activities throughout the healthcare supply chain. Table 4.2 provides details of these metrics that intend to evaluate the efficiency and effectiveness of sourcing, making, delivery, and selling processes of healthcare services.

Among the various supply chain performance metrics listed in Table 4.2, cash-to-cash cycle time can emerge as a more meaningful measure since it can help the healthcare organization to assess how lean its supply chain operations are with regard to its operating capital (cash at hand) in times of healthcare financial crisis. This measure also reflects the healthcare organization's ability to get engaged in a greater number of

Table 4.2 Healthcare supply chain performance metrics

Performance category	Performance metrics	Examples
Reliability: The performance of the supply chain in delivering the correct healthcare product or service, to the correct place, at the correct time, in the correct condition, in the correct quantity, with the correct documentation, to the correct patient or medical professional.	Delivery schedule	On-time delivery of medical supplies and pharmaceuticals; a measure of fulfilling patient demand by the designated deadline.
	Order fulfillment rate	A percentage of health are orders satisfied from available healthcare providers or medical supplies and medicines at hand; a percentage of prescription drug orders delivered on time and in full without quality failures or missing required documentation.
Responsiveness: The velocity at which a supply chain provides healthcare services or healthcare products to the patient.	Order cycle (lead) time	A summation of order processing and healthcare service delivery time.
Flexibility: The agility of a supply chain in responding to changes in healthcare demand or rules to gain or maintain competitive advantage.	Response time	Patient waiting time; a summation of patient call response time, emergency vehicle deployment time, and hospital admission time.
	Service flexibility	A measure of how quickly hospital capacity including available beds, medical doctors, and nurses can be adjusted to changing patient demand.
Cost: The costs associated with healthcare supply chain operations.	Total supply chain costs	A summation of all the costs associated with sourcing, making, delivery, and selling healthcare products and/or services.
Asset utilization: The effectiveness of a healthcare organization in managing assets to support patient satisfaction. This includes the	Cash-to-cash cycle time	A measure of how long it takes to convert a dollar spent on healthcare services to cash in hand.

(Continued)

Table 4.2 Healthcare supply chain performance metrics (Contiuned)

Performance category	Performance metrics	Examples
management of all assets such as fixed assets and working capital.	Inventory turnover	A measure of how long the inventory level of a certain healthcare product (e.g., medical supplies, devices, and pharmaceuticals) will be sufficient to match the expected patient demand.
	Asset turns	The total amount of revenue generated for every dollar's worth of assets managed by the healthcare organization; hospital bed utilization; medical equipment utilization.

value-adding activities with available cash that can be invested in those activities. In other words, the faster cash-to-cash cycle time could improve the bottom line of the healthcare organization.

4.3   Balanced Scorecard Approach

Over the years, financial measures such as a profit margin and annual revenue growth have been used in practice extensively to monitor the organization's performances. However, those measures often led the organization to focus on its short-term performance that does not necessarily reflect the organization's true operating efficiencies and thus cannot tell its long-term competitiveness. To overcome this shortcoming of the traditional financial measures, Kaplan and Norton (1992) introduced the concept of a balanced scorecard (BSC) that could supplement traditional financial measures with criteria that measure organizational performances from three additional perspectives: customers, internal business processes, and innovation and learning. In other words, BSC moderates the overemphasis on financial measures by including measures related to the underlying drivers of the long-term success. These measures are (1) patient perception of value; (2) internal processes and their outputs; (3) healthcare organization's ability to learn, grow, and evolve; and (4) financial gains obtained from these three drivers (DeBusk et al. 2003). This BSC concept can be modified to develop the basic framework of healthcare performance metrics. The details of these metrics within the BSC framework are summarized in Table 4.3 along with their potential illustrative measures. To develop a meaningful BSC that provides a balanced portfolio of the supply chain performance, these processes have to all be linked together and closely tied to healthcare supply chain activities. Thus, the BSC framework aligned with the goals and performance measures of healthcare supply chain practices are depicted in Figure 4.2. By incorporating the supply chain goals and performance measures into the BSC framework, we can develop a balanced scorecard framework intended for measuring the healthcare supply chain performance. This is shown in Figure 4.3.

Table 4.3 A summary of the four perspectives of the healthcare balanced scorecard

Perspective	Illustrative measures
Patient: The strategic priority for creating or adding patient value and service differentiation from the perspective of the patient	Patient satisfaction level, patient retention rate, new patient acquisition, patient defection rate, frequency of patient complaints, frequency of malpractice lawsuits, emergency response time
Internal healthcare organization: The strategic priorities for various business processes that create patient and healthcare stakeholder satisfaction	Healthcare worker productivity, medical equipment utilization, bed utilization, frequency of medical errors (or misdiagnosis), medical waste reduction, work flow efficiency
Innovation and learning: The strategic priority for continuous improvement of human capital through training and educational opportunities	Healthcare worker skill level, healthcare professional training hours, nurse or doctor (voluntary) turnover ratio
Financial gain: The strategic priority for revenue growth, profitability, improved bottom-line results, and mitigated risk from the perspective of healthcare service providers	Operating income, return-on-investment in medical facility or equipment, medical asset (e.g., medical equipment) utilization, and percentage of claims paid

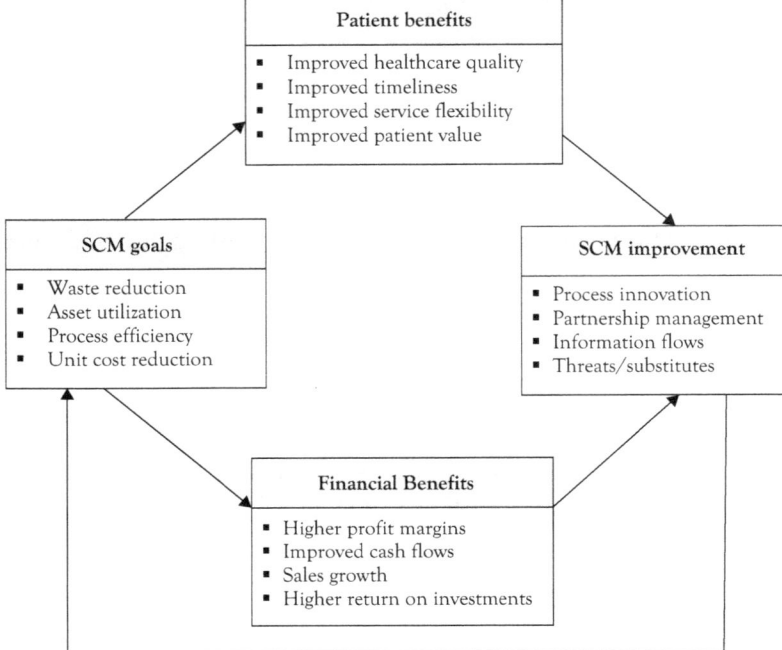

Figure 4.2 The strategic goals and performance measures of supply chain management

Source: Adapted and modified from Brewer and Speh (2000), p. 78.

As illustrated in Figure 4.3, each perspective of the supply chain BSC framework has different sets of goals and performance measures. Some of these goals and their related performance measures may be relevant to a certain medical setting in a certain healthcare organization (for example, hospital), but may be irrelevant to others (like a pharmaceutical manufacturer or healthcare insurance company). In other words, the supply chain BSC framework has to be tailored to specific needs and the surrounding environments of a particular organization and its supply chain partners. With that in mind, to better utilize the supply chain BSC framework, the following steps need to be taken:

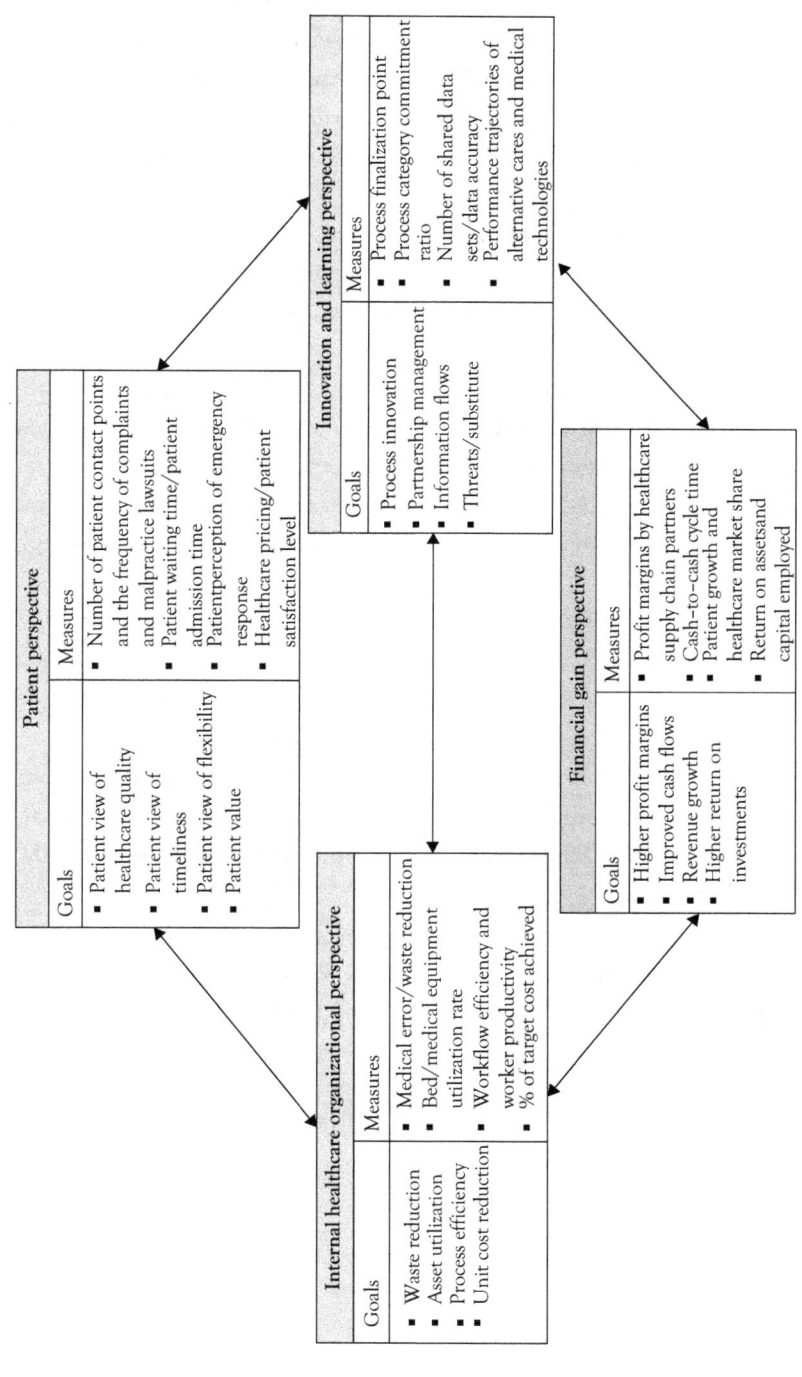

Figure 4.3 A healthcare supply chain balanced scorecard framework

Source: Adapted and modified from Brewer and Speh (2000), p. 86.

1. Plot the healthcare organization's future competitive position and formulate a supply chain strategy that allows the healthcare organization and its supply chain partners to achieve that position.
2. Translate this strategy into specific goals or objectives and measures that can be classified within each of the four perspectives of the BSC framework.
3. Set achievable targets for each measure.
4. Identify and develop courses of action (or initiatives) and then allocate necessary resources to such courses of action to reach those targets.
5. Monitor the performances of these courses of action, identify performance gaps, and then communicate the outcomes of these courses of action to internal customers (e.g., nurses, doctors, lab technicians) and external stakeholders (e.g., employers and payers, governments, insurers) within the organization and across the supply chain.
6. Develop specific plans to reduce performance gaps and then link the balanced scorecard to employees and supply chain partners (like suppliers) to their performance evaluation and reward (for example, merit pay, bonus, promotion, long-term contracts).
7. Readjust targets to changing patient demand and market positions, while continuously monitoring and improving the supply chain performance within each of the four perspectives of the BSC framework.

Based on the previous discussion, Figure 4.4 illustrates how the healthcare organization such as a hospital can develop its own BSC framework.

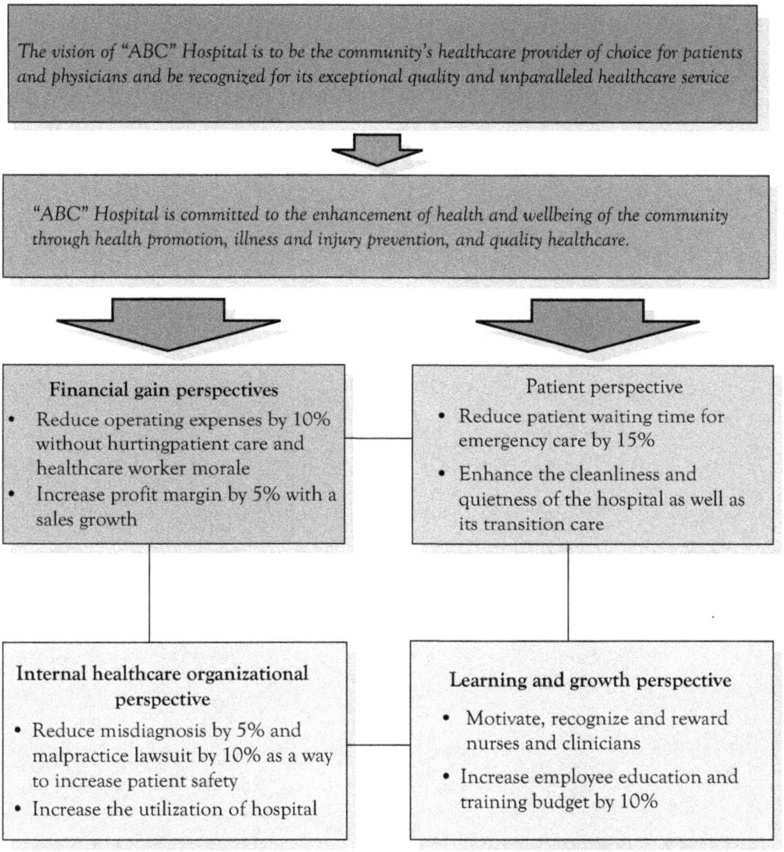

> The vision of "ABC" Hospital is to be the community's healthcare provider of choice for patients and physicians and be recognized for its exceptional quality and unparalleled healthcare service

> "ABC" Hospital is committed to the enhancement of health and wellbeing of the community through health promotion, illness and injury prevention, and quality healthcare.

Financial gain perspectives
- Reduce operating expenses by 10% without hurtingpatient care and healthcare worker morale
- Increase profit margin by 5% with a sales growth

Patient perspective
- Reduce patient waiting time for emergency care by 15%
- Enhance the cleanliness and quietness of the hospital as well as its transition care

Internal healthcare organizational perspective
- Reduce misdiagnosis by 5% and malpractice lawsuit by 10% as a way to increase patient safety
- Increase the utilization of hospital

Learning and growth perspective
- Motivate, recognize and reward nurses and clinicians
- Increase employee education and training budget by 10%

Figure 4.4 An illustrative example of the BSC framework for a hypothetical hospital

CHAPTER 5

Emerging Trends of Healthcare Supply Chain Management

As healthcare continues to evolve, its supply chain has to be transformed to adapt to changing healthcare environments. Some notable drivers for the transformation of healthcare supply chain practices include: advances in healthcare communication and information technology, globalization of the healthcare marketplace, and reforms in regulatory policy governing healthcare coverage and insurance. For instance, with an increase for more patient-centric care, today's patients seek for health interventions tailored to their individual needs, schedules, and affordability. Such patient-centric care can be facilitated by the greater access to real-time information through electronic health records (EHRs), telemedicine, electronic data interchange (EDI), and Internet media. Also, with a greater emphasis on preventive care, the healthcare industry's pendulum is swinging away from disease and injury treatments to wellness and fitness improvements. In response to these emerging trends, we should have a better understanding of what will drive healthcare supply chain practices in the future and how those drivers will shape up the patient's future healthcare behaviors and the healthcare provider's decision-making processes. With this in mind, the next sections will discuss about the role of information and communication technology (ICT) in the healthcare supply chain and then assess the impact of the global healthcare marketplace on the patient's healthcare behaviors and the healthcare provider's healthcare delivery practices.

5.1   Technological Evolution for Managing Healthcare Supply Chains

To cope with the rising healthcare cost, many healthcare organizations made conscious efforts to improve their productivity. One of the best ways to improve productivity is innovation. This innovation can be managerial and technical. Since the adoption of supply chain principles represents managerial innovation, its positive impact on the continuous improvement of healthcare will be magnified with the addition of technical innovation. In other words, the marriage of both managerial and technical innovation will create synergies for the continuous improvement of healthcare productivity. In the last few years, we have witnessed the emergence of new technologies that can revolutionize healthcare services and related supply chain activities. These are as follows:

1. *Mobile telecommunication technology*: This technology allows the healthcare provider to transmit time-sensitive data regarding the latest diagnosis, test results, patient's genomic composition, and biometric conditions (e.g., blood pressure, glucose level, and spirometer reading) to the patient's mobile devices (e.g., smart phone) on a real-time basis and thus helps reduce the number of unnecessary visits to the doctor's office and emergency room. That is to say, a greater use of mobile technology will lead to not only an increase in the patient's convenience level, but also the better utilization of the healthcare provider's resources (e.g., shorter waiting time at the doctor's office, reduced ambulance deployment) and the subsequent improvement of productivity.

2. *Wearable technology*: The recent advances in wearable sensors (e.g., Google Glass) allow the medical doctor to access to the live streaming of patient data (e.g., medical history) while interacting with the patient and his or her relatives. In particular, this kind of technology can be useful for reducing medical error during the surgery by offering the opportunity for intraoperative consultations and remote surgical mentoring.

3. *Electronic health record (EHR)*: EHR is a digital version of a patient's chart that contains a patient's medical history, diagnoses, medications,

treatment plans, immunization dates, allergies, radiology images, and laboratory test results. It also allows the clinician access to evidence-based tools that he or she can utilize to make right decisions about a patient's care, while automating and streamlining the clinician's workflow (HealthIT.gov 2014). Thus, EHR gives an opportunity for the clinician to see what kind of quality of care he or she provides to his or her patient.

4. *Three-dimensional (3D) printing*: 3D printing is the additive manufacturing process of producing a 3D solid copy of the object by laying down successive layers of materials based on digital technology. The potential application of 3D printing technology to healthcare is almost limitless. Indeed, the 3D printing market for healthcare is expected to grow more than $4.03 billion by 2018 (Visiongain 2014). 3D printing technology allows the healthcare provider to develop prototype medical models, stem cells, implants, dental products, bio tissues (e.g., heart tissue, skin tissue, and blood vessels), replacement organs (including cartilage and bones) and so forth, and thus enables the healthcare provider to save surgery time or cost and customize its care.

5. *Robotics*: Although applications of robotic technology for healthcare are still in its infancy, it has a wide application potential. In particular, surgical operations that require precision, durability, and repeatability will be good targets for the use of robotic technology that can automate surgical tasks and minimize invasive surgical procedures. Robots also can monitor the patient's medical conditions and recovery progress by checking on patients in different hospital rooms and managing their individual medical charts and vital signs without direct human intervention (MacRae 2013).

Regardless of numerous benefit potentials of the aforementioned technologies, their successful applications hinge on the smooth coordination and synchronization of these technologies across the healthcare supply chain processes and incorporate those into systematic decision-aid tools. The next section will discuss ways to leverage these technological innovations for efficient and effective healthcare supply chain management.

5.2   Intelligent Decision Support Systems for Healthcare Supply Chain Management

Unlike other decision areas, healthcare-related decisions such as clinical diagnosis and drug prescription require little or no margin for error since those decisions can be life-or-death matters. Recognizing this unique aspect of healthcare-related decisions, the healthcare organization needs to develop systematic decision-aid tools that can minimize human error with multiple layers of foolproof mechanism. One of such tools may be the intelligent decision support system (IDSS). In a broad sense, IDSS is an interactive decision-aid tool for solving well-structured problems that use artificial intelligence (AI) techniques (e.g., rule-based expert systems, neural networks, and pattern recognition) as well as computer-aided analytic techniques (e.g., operations research) to improve the quality of decision-making processes through learning and reasoning (see, e.g., Buckner and Shah 1991; Gottinger and Weimann 1992; Guerlain et al. 2000). An IDSS induces specific domain knowledge from raw data by identifying and extracting strategically useful information patterns from this data, thus making the extracted patterns understandable and usable for decision making. Unlike an ordinary decision support system, IDSS allows for supporting a wider range of decisions including those with uncertainty and retrieves information learned from past experiences, creates domain knowledge from recalled information, and translates it into new domain knowledge, thereby serving as a predictive tool (Basu et al. 2012). Before building the IDSS architecture, one should first understand what the typical decision-making sequences are in rendering healthcare services. For illustrative purposes, Figure 5.1 shows how decision sequences are made in the hospital setting. Since some of these sequences are repetitive and routine, decisions related to these sequences can be aided by the IDSS. For example, the medical check-up procedure routinely involves a dialog with the patient, physical examination (e.g., blood pressure and heart rate), laboratory tests, X-rays (including MRI), and other physician-ordered examinations (e.g., endoscopy). Thus, this routine procedure can be incorporated into the IDSS for error-free clinical decisions.

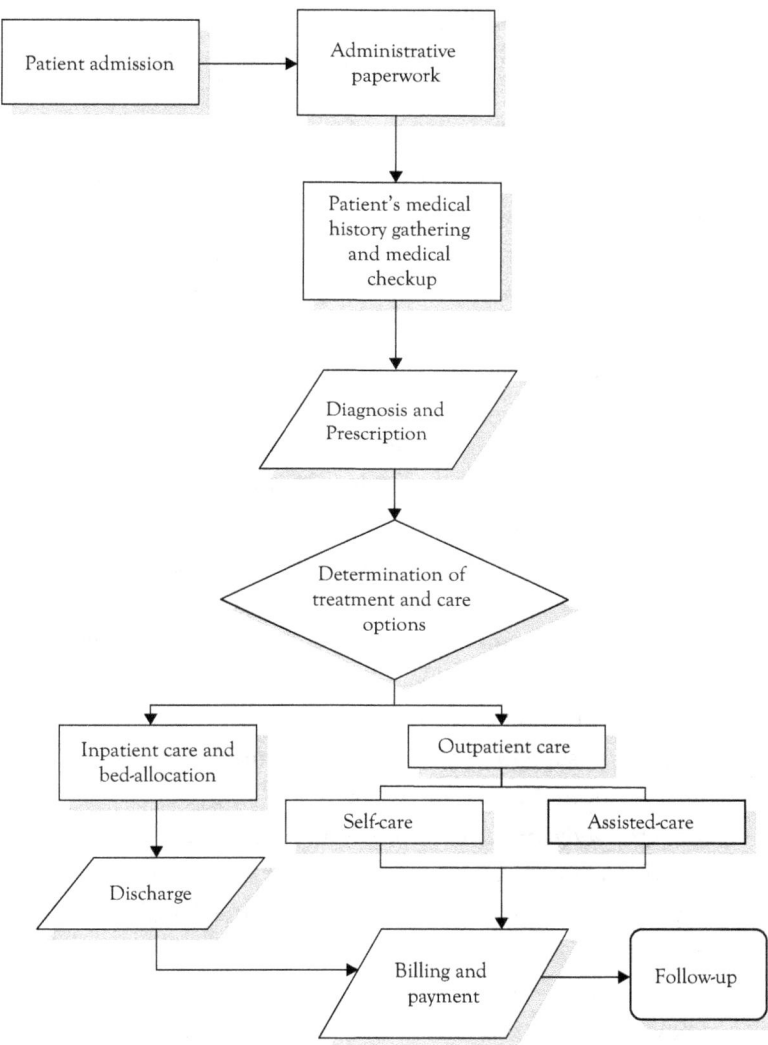

Figure 5.1 Hospital decision-making sequence

IDSS has wide application potentials for managing healthcare services and supply chains. Examples of potential IDSS application areas include: medical diagnosis, surveillance of infectious disease outbreaks, medication prescription, clinical intervention through medical warning signals, patient monitoring, and pathology ordering. Although the IDSS architecture should vary depending on a particular healthcare decision, its basic components of the architecture would be similar. Generally, the basic components of the healthcare IDSS comprise the following:

- *Databases* supported by a decision-oriented data repository such as the data warehouse.
- *Model bases* that aim to evaluate decision alternatives using analytical techniques such as operations research (OR), statistical analysis, simulation, and heuristic algorithms.
- *Case bases* that summarize practical guidelines for handling various instances of medical problems. The case bases should be able to retrieve the most similar case or cases, reuse the information and knowledge in that case to solve the problem, revise the proposed solution, and retain the parts of this experience to be useful for future problem solving (Aamodt and Plaza 1994).
- *Knowledge bases* that accumulate, transfer, and convert human expertise into meaningful knowledge through learning, reasoning, and improvement;
- *Dialog bases* supported by user interfaces and interactive feedback from the decision maker.
- *Intelligent advisory mechanism* that interprets and explains knowledge discovered by the analysis and then helps a decision maker suggest future courses of action based on the predicted decision outcomes.
- *Relevant software* including the model-based management software (MBMS) and data-based management software (DBMS).

Figure 5.2 graphically displays the generic architecture of the Healthcare IDSS that links the aforementioned components.

5.3   The Emergence of Medical Tourism

Spurred by spiraling healthcare expenses in developed countries and rapid globalization of the healthcare marketplace, medical tourism is on

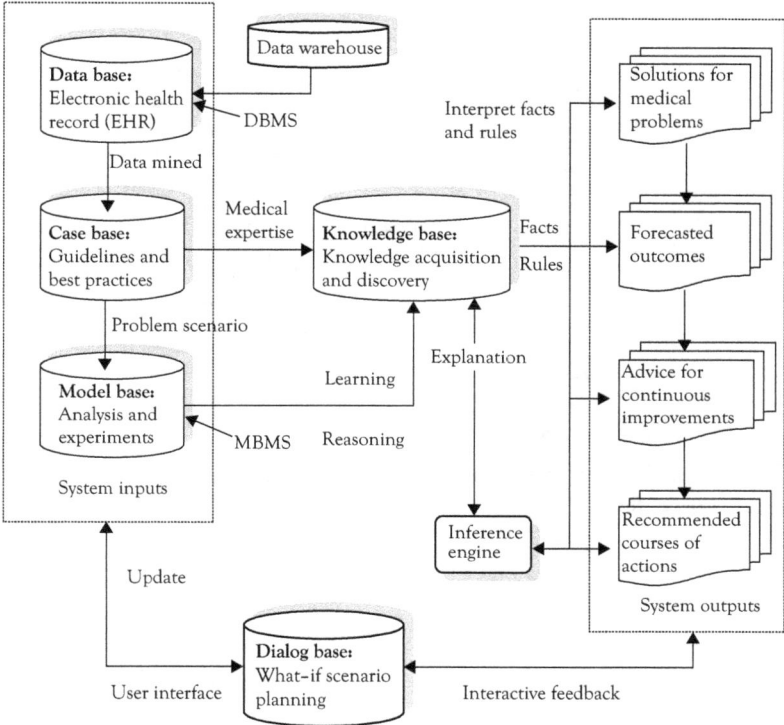

Figure 5.2 The architecture of the healthcare IDSS

the rise. According to Transparency Market Research (2013), the global medical tourism market was estimated to be US$10.5 billion in 2012 and is expected to reach a market worth US$32.5 billion in 2019 at an annual growth rate of 17.9 percent from 2013 to 2019. Medical tourism is generally referred to as the act of patients traveling from their home country to another country for the purpose of receiving better medical treatment, improved fitness, and alternative care. As shown in Figure 5.3, it generates a host of benefits for its users and providers. These benefits boosted medical tourism. These include: a greater affordability of medical care in developing countries (e.g., India and Mexico), the avoidance of long waiting times for certain medical procedures (e.g., long waits for hip replacement surgery in Canada), legal restrictions of certain medical procedures (e.g., fertility treatments), and a higher quality of specialty care (e.g., cosmetic surgery in South Korea). Among

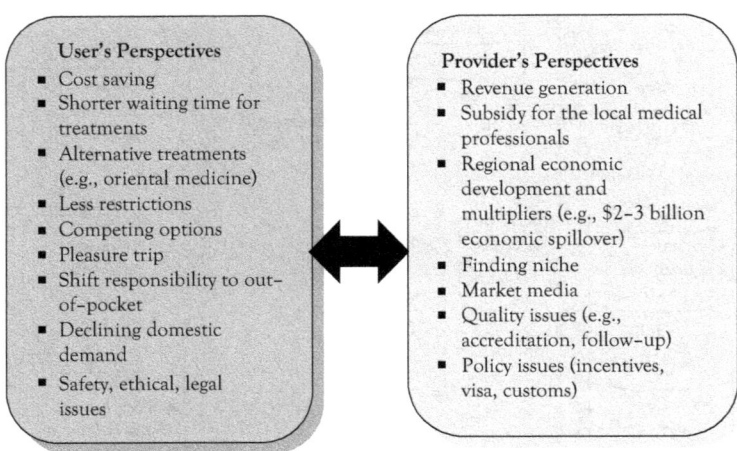

Figure 5.3 Perspectives of medical tourists and medical tourism service providers

others, a wide discrepancy in healthcare costs between different countries is one of the primary reasons for the increased popularity of medical tourism. For example, the cost of replacing a heart valve is estimated to be approximately $15,000 in India as compared to $150,000 in the United States. The heart bypass surgery can cost a patient a maximum of up to $144,000 in the United States, whereas it can only cost $26,000 on an average in Korea (Medical Tourism Resource Guide 2013). As a matter of fact, patients traveling abroad can save from 30 percent to 90 percent on the same or comparable medical procedure, including their travel expenditures, as compared to healthcare costs in their own countries (Transparency Market Research 2013). Average ranges of medical cost savings by the top destination countries are: Brazil, 25 to 40 percent; Costa Rica, 40 to 65 percent; India, 65 to 90 percent; Korea, 30 to 45 percent; Malaysia, 65 to 80 percent; Mexico, 40 to 65 percent; Singapore, 30 to 45 percent; Taiwan, 40 to 55 percent; Thailand, 50 to 70 percent; and Turkey, 50 to 65 percent (Health Travel Media 2011). In addition to cost-saving opportunities, many of these destination countries for medical tourism are known for excellence in certain specialty care as summarized in Table 5.1 (see, e.g., Snow 2013). The origins of this medical tourism are typically wealthy developed countries such as

Table 5.1 Top destinations for medical tourism and their specialty cares

Destination	Specialty cares
India	Orthopedic and cardiac surgery
Korea	Cosmetic (e.g., face lift and corrective) surgery, cancer and spinal treatments
Malaysia	Health screening (e.g., vision, dental, hearing, MRI, and PET scan)
Singapore	Cancer and stem-cell (e.g., Alzheimer's and Parkinson's) treatments
Thailand	Cosmetic and transgender reassignment surgery
Croatia	Superlative care, rehabilitation and wellness treatments, dental care, eye treatments
Hungary	Dental care (e.g., implant and crown molding)
Turkey	Cardiac, orthopedic, laser eye surgery and cancer treatments
Antigua	Drug addiction treatment and recovery
Barbados	Fertility treatments
Brazil	Cosmetic surgery
Costa Rica	Dental care
Mexico	Bariatric (e.g., weight loss, lap band, and gastric bypass) and cosmetic surgery
South Africa	Cardiac and cosmetic surgery
Israel	Fertility treatments
Australia	Skin cancer

the United States, Canada, the United Kingdom, and the European Union (EU) where the medical costs are relatively high and long waits for medical treatments are common.

Also, the medical tourism is facilitated by the host country's travel support including sightseeing attractions, hotel accommodations, and logistical access. Since the medical tourism typically involves activities of acquisition (e.g., buying foreign healthcare services) and logistics (e.g., traveling), it has supply chain ramifications. Figure 5.4 shows typical routines of the medical tourism process. In particular, the first two steps of this process are crucial for the successful medical tour because many patients are unfamiliar with the foreign medical system and statutes (e.g., privacy laws) not to mention potential patient safety issues. As such, the role of medical tourism facilitator is increasing. The medical

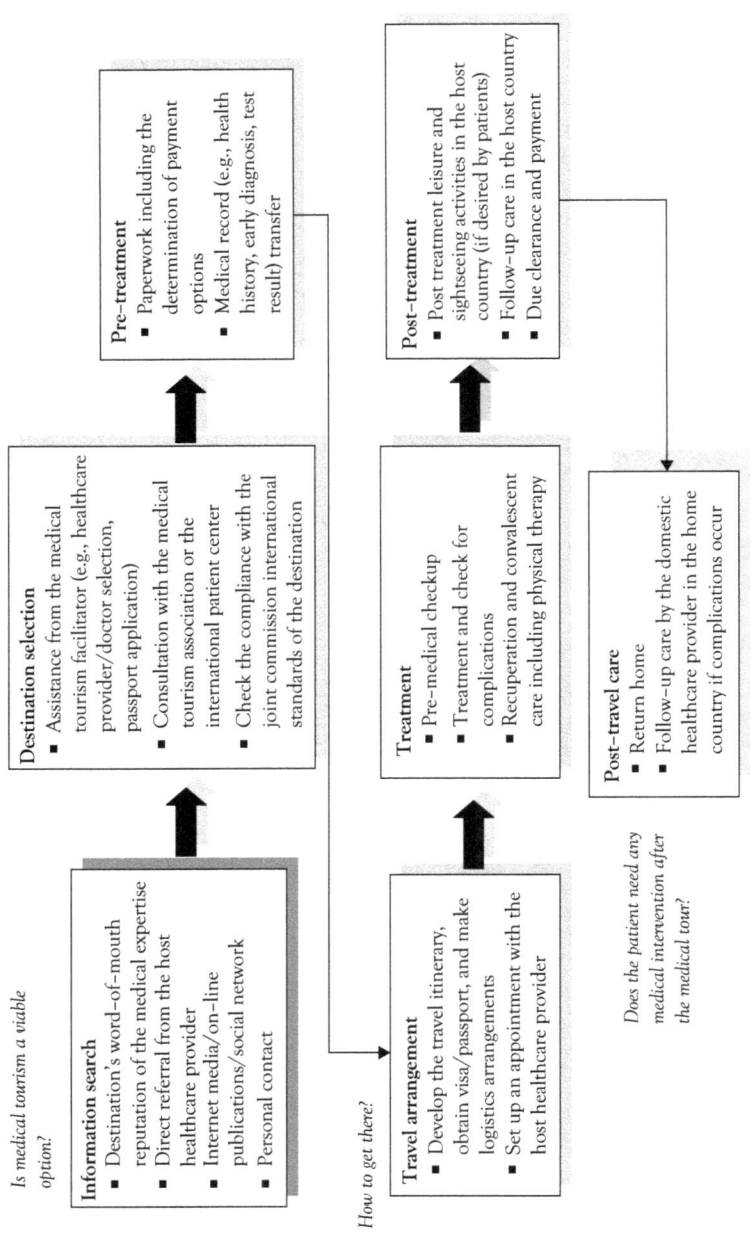

Information search
- Destination's word-of-mouth reputation of the medical expertise
- Direct referral from the host healthcare provider
- Internet media/on-line publications/social network
- Personal contact

Is medical tourism a viable option?

Destination selection
- Assistance from the medical tourism facilitator (e.g., healthcare provider/doctor selection, passport application)
- Consultation with the medical tourism association or the international patient center
- Check the compliance with the joint commission international standards of the destination

Pre-treatment
- Paperwork including the determination of payment options
- Medical record (e.g., health history, early diagnosis, test result) transfer

How to get there?

Travel arrangement
- Develop the travel itinerary, obtain visa/passport, and make logistics arrangements
- Set up an appointment with the host healthcare provider

Treatment
- Pre-medical checkup
- Treatment and check for complications
- Recuperation and convalescent care including physical therapy

Post-treatment
- Post treatment leisure and sightseeing activities in the host country (if desired by patients)
- Follow-up care in the host country
- Due clearance and payment

Does the patient need any medical intervention after the medical tour?

Post-travel care
- Return home
- Follow-up care by the domestic healthcare provider in the home country if complications occur

Figure 5.4 The medical tourism process

tourism facilitator can guide patients through the process of securing patient safety and assuring acceptable healthcare quality and affordable treatments and tours. However, it should be noted that the medical tourism facilitator charges a referral fee as its commission for serving as a liaison between the patient and the host healthcare provider. Although this kind of commission is justifiable, some facilitators can inflate the price and direct the patient toward certain healthcare providers while committing frauds. Thus, caution should be exercised in selecting the medical tourism facilitator, because it can be the weakest link in the medical tourism supply chain.

In addition to the aforementioned challenges, medical tourism can pose some serious health threats and statutory risks. These threats and risks include: the spreads of infectious diseases or multidrug-resistant germs across the countries through more frequent travels, increased health risk associated with commercial organ transplantations and unproven stem cell treatments, and potential legal or ethical violations (e.g., assisted suicide, premature abortion, and surrogacy) associated with unconventional medical procedures (e.g., disruptions of continuum of medical care, a lack of privacy protection, and limited recourse for postoperative complications).

5.4   Blueprints for the Futuristic Healthcare Supply Chain

An individual's health directly affects the quality of his or her life. As such, healthcare takes the center stage for the nation's effort to improve its welfare or well-being. Despite such efforts, the current status of healthcare across the world raises some serious concerns. These concerns include: healthcare inequities resulting from the unaffordable cost of healthcare services, a chronic shortage of healthcare professionals, regional price disparities for medical treatments and pharmaceuticals, medical waste controls and disposals, proliferation of fake and substandard drugs, globalization of healthcare services, limited healthcare access caused by logistical complexity, and added managerial challenges posed by rapid technological advances. Although this book has attempted to address these concerns in earlier chapters and sections, we have to be aware that our ability to handle these concerns will shape up the future of healthcare. With this in mind, let us raise a list of specific questions that we need to answer to develop the futuristic healthcare supply chain.

1. How to control the cost of healthcare throughout its entire supply chain? (How to identify and eliminate non-value-adding activities throughout the healthcare supply chain processes?)
2. How to continuously improve the quality of healthcare (especially primary care)? (What are the primary sources of healthcare quality failures? What is needed to reduce the likelihood of medical error or malpractices or wrong prescriptions?)
3. How to reduce healthcare inequity gaps among people of different economic status, age, race, gender, nationality, and cultural or educational backgrounds? (How to make healthcare more affordable or accessible to every citizen?)
4. How to comply with changing healthcare laws, regulations, and accreditation mandates? (Which stipulations and mandates are game changers? What changes are needed to meet changing healthcare rules and standards?)
5. How to cope with the globalization of the healthcare marketplace? (How to deal with the increased complexity and risk associated with the stretched global healthcare supply chain? What will the impact of medical tourism be on healthcare pricing and service delivery?)
6. How to make healthcare providers more competitive in the more crowded healthcare market? (What will it to take to enhance the competitive edge of healthcare providers over their rivals? How to evaluate the relative performances of healthcare service providers?)
7. How to embrace and exploit advances in information and communication technology (ICT) to improve healthcare deliveries? (What are the most appropriate application areas for ICT? What will be the expected benefits and costs of ICT for healthcare? What are the biggest barriers to ICT implementation for healthcare?)
8. How to build a long-term partnership with other healthcare stakeholders to share resources and risks to make the healthcare supply chain more resilient from unexpected disruptions? (Who will be considered right supply chain partners? What attributes are most important for selecting the right partner?)

Although no single remedy can answer all of these questions, the following traits may represent the most desirable prerequisite for the futuristic healthcare supply chain:

1. *Patient-centric*: ability to sustain more interactive patient-healthcare professional (e.g., doctor and nurse) relationship.
2. *Time-sensitive*: ability to respond to the patient's needs without unnecessary delays and bring the medical attention to him or her immediately. That is to say, the focus of the healthcare supply chain should be directed to its agility by eliminating redundant or duplicated healthcare procedures and adopting lean principles (including just-in-time philosophy) throughout the supply chain.
3. *Real-time information sharing*: ability to share the accurate information with patients or other healthcare stakeholders in a timely manner (especially on a real-time basis) helps healthcare professionals make a right decision for time-sensitive treatments. As such, the role of electronic healthcare records as well as mobile (or hand-held) technology in the healthcare supply chain will be increased.
4. *Foolproof*: ability to mitigate healthcare risks including medical error, prescription mistakes, supply chain disruptions (e.g., shortages or delayed deliveries of medical supplies or devices), and lagging patient safety with the built-in system (e.g., less human involvement, automated, and computer-aided).
5. *Traceable*: ability to track the sources (or root causes) of problems (e.g., counterfeit drugs and recalls of tainted drugs) can increase patient safety and the subsequent quality of care. As such, RFID technology should be exploited more for managing the pharmaceutical supply chain across the globe.
6. *Scalable*: ability to deal with an increased demand of healthcare from a certain demographic sector such as the older generation or formerly uninsured individuals. Also, this ability will help create economies of scale and thus help reduce the cost of care.
7. *Collaborative*: ability to work with other stakeholders to share the burden of providing healthcare services. In particular, the continued and expanded exploitation of collaborative purchasing will be crucial for controlling the rising expenditures associated with the acquisition and replenishment of essential medical supplies, equipment, and drugs.

In addition, it is reminded that given that the futuristic healthcare supply chain cannot settle with status-quo, the healthcare organization's ability to adapt to managerial changes is paramount for the successful transformation of healthcare practices. In other words, nurturing change management skills for healthcare decision or policy makers should precede any effort to innovate healthcare processes.

References

Aamodt, A., and E. Plaza. 1994. "Case-Based Reasoning: Foundational Issues, Methodological Variations, and System Approaches." *Artificial Intelligence Communications* 7, no. 1, pp. 39–59.

Al-Shallash, K., and M. Shereif. 2007. "Healthcare Waste Management in Saudi Arabia: A Case Study." *Proceedings of the 10th International Conference on Environmental Science and Technology*, pp. 24–27. Kos Island, Greece.

Altarum Institute. 2011. *Strategic Innovations for Affordable, Sustainable Healthcare: A Model for Health System Reform*, Unpublished Report, Ann Arbor, MI: Altarum Institute.

Anderson, G.F. 2007. "From 'Soak the Rich' to 'Soak the Poor': Recent Trends in Hospital Pricing." *Health Affairs* 26, no. 3, pp. 780–789.

Atella, V., E. Schafheutle, P. Noyce, and K. Hassell. 2005. "Affordability of Medicines and Patients' Cost-Reducing Behavior." *Applied Health Economics and Health Policy* 4, no. 1, pp. 23–35.

Averboukh, E.A. April 2006. "Six Sigma Trends: Six Sigma in Financial Services." *TRIZ Journal*, pp. 1–10.

Bacheldor, B. August 28, 2007. "GlaxoSmithKline Remains Committed to RFID," *RFID Journal*, http://www.rfidjournal.com/articles/view?3584, (accessed February 14, 2014).

Ballou, R.H., Gilbert, S.M. and Mukherjee, A. 2000. "New managerial challenges from supply chain opportunities," *Industrial Marketing Management*, vol. 29, 7–18.

Basu, R., N. Archer, and B. Mukherjee. 2012. "Intelligent Decision Support in Healthcare." *Analytics: INFORMS*, http://www.analytics-magazine. org/januaryfebruary-2012/507-intelligent-decision-support-in-healthcar, (accessed February 26, 2014).

Beckman, H.B., K.M. Markakis, A.L. Suchman, and R.M. Frankel. 1994. "The Doctor-Patient Relationship and Malpractice: Lessons from Plaintiff Depositions." *Archives of Internal Medicine* 154, no. 12, pp. 1365–1370.

Bell, S.J., G.J. Whitewall, and B.A. Lukas. 2002. "Schools of Thought in Organizational Learning." *Academy of Marketing Science* 30, no. 1, pp. 70–86.

Berkley, H.R. 2014. "Who is Considered a Healthcare Provider/Practitioner?" *FAQ*, http://hrweb.berkeley.edu/faq/1178, (accessed February 7, 2014).

Boland, P. 1996. "The Role of Reengineering in Healthcare Delivery." *Managed Care Quarterly* 4, no. 4, p. 1.

Bolstorff, P. and Rosenbaum, R. 2003. *Supply Chain Excellence: A Handbook for Dramatic Improvement Using the SCOR Model*, New York, NY: AMACOM.

Braithwaite, A., and D. Hall. 1999. "Risky Business: Critical Decisions in Supply Chain Management." *Logistics Consulting Partners.* Hertfordshire, United Kingdom: LCP Ltd.

Brewer, P., and T. Speh. 2000. "Using the Balanced Scorecard to Measure Supply Chain Performance." *Journal of Business Logistics* 21, no. 1, pp. 78–86.

Brotcorne, L., G. Laporte, and F. Semet. 2003. "Ambulance Location and Relocation Models." *European Journal of Operational Research* 147, no. 3, pp. 451–463.

Buckner, G., and V. Shah. 1991. "Intelligent Decision Support Systems." *Journal of Computer Information Systems* 31, no. 2, pp. 61–65.

Burns, L.R., R.A. DeGraaff, P.M. Danzon, J.R. Kimberly, W.L. Kissick, and M.V. Pauly. 2002. "The Wharton School Study of the Healthcare Value Chain." In *The Healthcare Value Chain: Producers, Purchasers and Providers*, pp. 3–26. San Francisco, CA: Jossey-Bass.

Burnson, P. April 1, 2013. "3PL Management: Conquering the Cold Chain." *Logistics Management*, http://www.logisticsmgmt.com/article/3pl_management_conquering_the_cold_chain, (accessed February 11, 2014).

Calvo, A.B., and D.H. Marks. 1973. "Location of Healthcare Facilities: An Analytical Approach." *Socio-Economic Planning Sciences* 7, no. 5, pp. 407–422.

Carr, A.S., M. Zhang, I. Klopping, and H. Min. 2010. "RFID Technology: Implications for Healthcare Organizations." *American Journal of Business* 25, no. 2, pp. 1–16.

Carroll, J.S., and A.C. Edmondson. 2002. "Leading Organizational Learning in Healthcare." *Quality and Safety in Healthcare* 11, no. 1, pp. 51–56.

CDC. 2012. *Early Release of Selected Estimates Based on Data From the 2011 National Health Interview Survey.* Unpublished Report, Hyattsville, MD: National Center for Health Statistics.

Chopra, S., and P. Meindl. 2004. *Supply Chain Management: Strategy, Planning and Operation.* Upper Saddle River, NJ: Prentice-Hall.

Chowdhury, S. 2001. *The Power of Six Sigma.* Upper Saddle River, NJ: Financial Times Prentice Hall.

Church, R., and C.R. ReVelle. 1974. "The Maximal Covering Location Problem." *Papers in Regional Science* 32, no. 1, pp. 101–118.

Chvatal, V. 1979. "A Greedy Heuristic for the Set-Covering Problem." *Mathematics of Operations Research* 4, no. 3, pp. 233–235.

Congressional Budget Office. 2011. *The Long-Term Budget Outlook.* Unpublished Report, Washington, DC: Congressional Budget Office.

Congressional Budget Office. March 11, 2010. "H.R. 3590, Patient Protection and Affordable Care Act," in Letter from Douglas W. Elmendorf, Congressional Budget Office Director, to the Honorable Harry Reid, Senate Majority Leader, Washington DC: Congressional Budget Office, http://www.cbo.gov/sites/default/files/cbofiles/ftpdocs/113xx/doc11307/reid_letter_hr3590.pdf

Cooper, M.C., D.M. Lambert, and J.D. Pagh. 1997b. "Supply Chain Management: More than a New Name for Logistics." *The International Journal of Logistics Management* 8, no. 1, pp. 1–13.

Czaja, S.J., and J. Sharit. 2009. "The Aging of the Population: Opportunities and Challenges for Human Factors Engineering." *The Bridge: Linking Engineering and Society* 39, no. 1, pp. 34–40.

Daskin, M. 1983. "The Maximal Expected Coveting Location Model: Formulation, Properties and Heuristic Solution." *Transportation Science* 17, no. 1, pp. 48–70.

Daskin, M.S., and E.H. Stern. 1981. "A Hierarchical Objective Set Covering Model for Emergency Medical Service Vehicle Deployment." *Transportation Science* 15, no. 2, pp. 137–152.

Daskin, M.S., and L.K. Dean. 2004. "Location of Healthcare Facilities." In *Operations Research and Healthcare: A Handbook of Methods and Applications (Vol. 70)* eds. M.L. Brandeau, F. Sainfort, W.P. Pierskalla, 43–76, Vol.70. Norwell, MA: Kluwer Academic Publlishers.

Davison, M. 2011. *Pharmaceutical Anti-Counterfeiting: Combating the Real Danger from Fake Drugs.* Hoboken, NJ: Wiley.

de la Maisonneuve, C., and J.O. Martins. 2013. *A Projection Method for Public Health and Long-term Care Expenditures*, Economics Department Working Papers, No. 1048, Paris, France: OECD.

DeBusk, G.K., R.M. Brown, and L.N. Killough. 2003. "Components and Relative Weights in Utilization of Dashboard Measurement Systems like the Balanced Scorecard." *British Accounting Review* 35, pp. 215–231.

Delaune, J., and W. Everett. 2008. *Clinical Care: A Comprehensive Analysis in Support of System-Wide Improvements*, Unpublished Report, Cambridge, MA: New England Healthcare Institute.

Dranove, D., W.D. White, and L. Wu. 1993. "Segmentation in Local Hospital Markets." *Medical Care* 31, no. 1, pp. 52–64.

Dukes, M.N.G., F.M. Haaijer-Ruskamp, C.P. de Joncheere, and A.H. Rietveld. 2003. *Drugs and Money: Prices, Affordability and Cost Containment.* Amsterdam, The Netherlands: IOC Press.

Eaton, D.J., M.S. Daskin, D. Simmons, B. Bulloch, and G. Jansma. 1985. "Determining Emergency Medical Service Vehicle Deployment in Austin, Texas." *Interfaces* 15, no. 1, pp. 96–108.

Ebel, T., E. Larsen, and K. Shah. September 2013. "Strengthening Healthcare's Supply Chain: A Five Step Plan." *McKinsey & Company Insights and Publications*, http://www.mckinsey.com/insights/health_systems_and_services /strengthening_health_cares_supply_chain_a_five_step_plan, (accessed January 22, 2014).

Eller, T. 2009. "Improve Patient Satisfaction Through Segmentation." *HFMA Show Me of Missouri Chapter: Healthcare Financial Association Newsletter,* http://www.hfmashowme.org/newsletters/Fall%202009%20Newsletter.pdf, (accessed January 25, 2014).

European Commission. 2014. "Eurostat Population Projections 2010–2060," http://www.airo.ie/news/europe-2060-population-projections-ireland-increase-465-interact-data, (accessed January 31, 2014).

Fiol, C.M., and M.A. Lyle. 1985. "Organizational Learning." *Academy of Management Review* 10, no. 4, pp. 803–813.

Fitzsimmons, J.A. 1973. "A Methodology for Emergency Ambulance Deployment." *Management Science* 19, no. 6, pp. 627–636.

Fowler, T.C. 1990. *Value Analysis in Design.* New York, NY: Van Nostrand Reinhold.

Fries, K.E. 2005. "Practical, Hands-on Change Management." *Presented at the 28th Annual WERC Conference*, Dallas, Texas.

Gardner, J.T., and M.C. Cooper. 2003. "Strategic Supply Chain Mapping Approaches." *Journal of Business Logistics* 24, no. 2, pp. 37–64.

Garvin, D. 2000. *Learning in Action: A Guide to Putting the Learning Organization to Work.* Boston, MA: Harvard Business School Press.

Generic Pharmaceutical Association. 2013. *Generic Drug Savings in the US*, Unpublished Report, Fifth annual edition, Washington, DC: Generic Pharmaceutical Association.

Gibson, B.J., J.T. Mentzer, and R.I. Cook. 2005. "Supply Chain Management: The Pursuit of a Consensus Definition." *Journal of Business Logistics* 26, no. 2, pp. 17–25.

Gobbi, C., and J. Hsuan. 2010. "Collaborative Purchasing in Healthcare System." *Proceedings of the Seventeenth International Annual EUROMA Conference: Managing Operations in Service Economies*, 7–9 June, Porto, Portugal, CEN.

Goldberg, J.B. 2004. "Operations Research Models for the Deployment of Emergency Services Vehicles." *EMS Management Journal* 1, no. 1, pp. 20–39.

Goldenberg, D.E., and R. King. 2009. *A 2008 Update of Cost Savings and a Marketplace Analysis of the Healthcare Group Purchasing Industry*, Unpublished Report, July, Laurel, MD: Locus Systems, Inc.

Goldman, T.R. July 31, 2012. "Eliminating Fraud and Abuse." *Health Policy Brief*, pp. 1–5.

Goldsby, T., and R. Martichenko. 2005., *Lean Six Sigma Logistics: Strategic Development to Operational Success.* Boca Raton, FL: J. Ross Publishing.

Gottinger, H.W., and P. Weimann. 1992. "Intelligent Decision Support Systems." *Decision Support Systems* 8, no. 4, pp. 317–332.

Greenemeir, L. November 4, 2008. "Heparin Scare: Deaths From Tainted Blood-Thinner Spur Race for Safe Replacement." *Scientific American*, http://www.scientificamerican.com/article/heparin-scare-deaths/, (accessed February 12, 2014).

Gröne, O., and M. Garcia-Barbero. 2001. "Integrated Care: A Position Paper of the WHO European Office for Integrated Healthcare Services." *International Journal of Integrated Care* 1, no. 1, p. e21.

Guerlain, S., D.E. Brown, and C. Mastrangelo. 2000. "Intelligent Decision Support Systems." *Proceedings of Systems, Man, and Cybernetics, 2000 IEEE International Conference* 3, pp. 1934–1938.

Harry, M.J., and R. Schroeder. 2006. *Six Sigma: The Breakthrough Management Strategy Revolutionizing the World's Top Corporations.* New York, NY: Random House Digital, Inc.

Hassan, M.M., S.A. Ahmed, K.A. Rahman, and T.K. Biswas. 2008. "Pattern of Medical Waste Management: Existing Scenario in Dhaka City, Bangladesh." *BMC Public Health* 8, no. 1, pp. 36–45.

Health Information and Quality Authority. 2013. *Guidance on Developing Key Performance Indicators (KPIs) and Minimum Data Sets to Monitor Healthcare Quality Version 1.1,* Unpublished Report, Cork, Ireland: HIQA.

Health Travel Media. 2011. *Patients Beyond Borders: Everybody's Guide to Affordable World-Class Healthcare,* Unpublished Report, Chapel Hill, NC: Patients Beyond Borders.

HealthIT.gov. 2014. "What is an electronic health record?" http://www.healthit .gov/providers-professionals/faqs/what-electronic-health-record-ehr, (accessed February 25, 2014).

Hendrick, T.E. 1997. *Purchasing Consortia: Horizontal Alliances among Firms Buying Common Goods and Services,* Unpublished Report, Temple, AZ: Centre for Advanced Purchasing Studies (CAPS).

Herring, A.A., A.A. Ginde, J. Fahimi, H.J. Alter, J.H. Maselli, J.A. Espinola, A.F. Sullivan, and C.A. Jr. Camargo. 2013. "Increasing Critical Care Admissions from U.S. Emergency Departments, 2001–2009." *Critical Care Medicine* 41, no. 5, pp. 1197–1204.

Herzlinger, R.E. 2002. "Let's Put Consumers in Charge of Healthcare." *Harvard Business Review* 80, no. 7, p. 44.

Hines, P., and N. Rich. 1997. "The Seven Value Stream Mapping Tools." *International Journal of Operations and Production Management* 17, no. 1, pp. 46–64.

Hughes, J., M. Ralif, and B. Michels. 1998. *Transform Your Supply Chain: Releasing Value in Business.* London, UK: Thomson Business Press.

Huntington, W.V., L.A. Covington, P.P. Center, L.A. Covington, and L. Manchikanti. 2011. "Patient Protection and Affordable Care Act of 2010: Reforming the Healthcare Reform for the New Decade." *Pain Physician* 14, pp. E35–E67.

Hurwitz, M.A. 1991. "Bundling Patented Drugs and Medical Services: An Antitrust Analysis." *Columbia Law Review* 91, no. 5, pp. 1188–1220.

IMS Health Incorporated. 2012. "Global Pharmaceutical Industry and Market." http://www.abpi.org.uk/industry-info/knowledge-hub/global-industry/Pages/industry-market-.aspx, (accessed February 12, 2014).

IMS Institute for Healthcare Informatics. 2012. *The Global Use of Medicines: Outlook through 2016*, Unpublished Report, Parsippany, NJ: IMS Health Incorporated.

Infosys. 2009. *KPIs for Effective, Real-Time Dashboards in Hospitals*, Unpublished White Paper, Bangalore, India: Infosys.

International Federation of Pharmaceutical Manufacturers and Associations. 2013. *Facts and Figures 2012*, Unpublished Report, Geneva, Switzerland: IFPMA.

Jimmerson, C. 2009. *Value Stream Mapping for Healthcare Made Easy*. Boca Raton, FL: CRC Press.

Jones, J.M. 2008. "Healthcare Access, Cost are Top Health Concerns: Majority Mention Either Access to or Cost of Healthcare as Most Urgent Health Problem." *Gallup's annual Health and Healthcare Poll*, http://www.gallup.com/poll/112516/healthcare-access-cost-top-health-concerns.aspx, (accessed February 8, 2014).

Kaiser Permanente. 2010. *Reducing Operating Room Waste with Sterile Wrap Recycling*, Unpublished Report, https://practicegreenhealth.org/sites/default/files/upload-files/sterile_wrap_recycling_success_story_4.10.pdf, (accessed February 20, 2014).

Kanavos, P., A. Ferrario, S. Vandoros, and G.F. Anderson. 2013. "Higher US Branded Drug Prices and Spending Compared to Other Countries May Stem Partly From Quick Uptake of New Drugs." *Health Affairs* 32, no. 4, pp. 753–761.

Kaplan, R.S. 2009. *Measuring Performance, Pocket Mentor Series*. Cambridge, MA: Harvard Business Press.

Kaplan, R.S. and Norton, D.P. 1992. The Balanced Scorecard - Measures that Drive Performance, Harvard Business Review (January-February), vol. 70, no. 1, pp. 71–79.

King, D.L., D.I. Ben-Tovim, and J. Bassham. 2006. "Redesigning Emergency Department Patient Flows: Application of Lean Thinking to Healthcare." *Emergency Medicine Australasia* 18, no. 4, pp. 391–397.

Koning, H., J.P. Verver, J. Heuvel, S. Bisgaard, and R.J. Does. 2006. "Lean Six Sigma in Healthcare." *Journal for Healthcare Quality* 28, no. 2, pp. 4–11.

Kotter, J.P. 1996. *Leading Change*. Boston, MA: Harvard Business School Press.

Kwon, I.G., and Suh, T. 2004. "Factors affecting the level of trust and commitment in supply chain relationships," *Journal of Supply Chain Management* 40, no.2, pp. 4–14.

Lambert, D.M., and C.M. Lewis. 1980. "Meaning, Measurement and Implementation of Customer Service." *Proceedings of the Annual Conference of the National Council of Physical Distribution Management*, pp. 524–602.

Landry, S., and R. Philippe. 2004. "How Logistics Can Service Healthcare." *Supply Chain Forum: An International Journal* 5, no. 2, pp. 26–76.

Lasa, I.S., C.O. Laburu, and R. de Castro Vila. 2008. "An Evaluation of the Value Stream Mapping Tool." *Business Process Management Journal* 14, no. 1, pp. 39–52.

Lee, H.L., V. Padmanabhan, and S. Whang. 1997a. "Information Distortion in a Supply Chain: The Bullwhip Effect." *Management Science* 43, no. 4, pp. 546–558.

Lee, H.L., V. Padmanabhan, and S. Whang. 1997b. "The Bullwhip Effect in Supply Chains." *Sloan Management Review* 38, no. 3, pp. 93–102.

Leenders, M.R., P.F. Johnson, A.E. Flynn, and H.E. Fearon. 2006. *Purchasing and Supply Management*. 13th ed. New York, NY: McGraw-Hill/Irwin.

Lieb, R., and J. Miller. 2002. "The Use of Third-Party Logistics Services by Large US Manufacturers, The 2000 Survey." *International Journal of Logistics: Research and Applications* 5, no. 1, pp. 1–12.

Lin, B., and J.A. Vassar. 1996. "Implications of Reengineering in Healthcare." *The Healthcare Manager* 15, no. 2, pp. 63–68.

López-Casasnovas, G., and J. Puig-Junoy. 2000. "Review of the Literature on Reference Pricing." *Health Policy* 54, no. 2, pp. 87–123.

Lummus, R.R., R.J. Vokurka, and B. Rodeghiero. 2006. "Improving Quality Through Value Stream Mapping: A Case Study of a Physician's Clinic." *Total Quality Management* 17, no. 8, pp. 1063–1075.

MacRae, M. 2013. "Top 5 Medical Technology Innovations." *ASME News*, https://www.asme.org/engineering-topics/articles/bioengineering/top-5-medical-technology-innovations, (accessed February 26, 2014).

Maltz, A.B., and L.M. Ellram. 2000. "Selling Inbound Logistics Services: Understanding the Buyer's Perspective," *Journal of Business Logistics* 21, no. 2, pp. 69–88.

Medical Tourism Resource Guide. 2013. *Medical Tourism in 2013, Facts and Statistics*, Unpublished Report, http://www.medicaltourismresourceguide.com/medical-tourism-in-2013, (accessed February 22, 2014).

MedlinePlus. 2014. "Types of Healthcare Providers." *Health Topics*, http://www.nlm.nih.gov/medlineplus/ency/article/001933.htm, (accessed February 7, 2014).

Melnick, G.A., and K. Fonkych. 2008. "Hospital Pricing and the Uninsured: Do the Uninsured Pay Higher Prices?" *Health Affairs* 27, no. 2, pp. 116–122.

Miles, L.D. 1972. *Techniques of Value Analysis and Engineering*, Vol. 4. New York, NY: McGraw-Hill.

Milken Institute. 2013. *An Unhealthy America: Economic Burden of Chronic Disease*, Unpublished Report, Santa Monica, CA: Milken Institute.

Min, H. 2000. "The Bullwhip Effect in Supply Chain Management." In *Encyclopedia of Production and Manufacturing Management*, eds. P. Swamidass, 66–70. Boston, MA: Kluwer Academic Publishers.

Min, H. 2012. "Mapping the Supply Chain of Anti-Malarial Drugs in Sub-Saharan African Countries." *International Journal of Logistics Systems and Management* 11, no. 1, pp. 1–23.

Min, H., and G. Zhou. 2002. "Supply Chain Modeling: Past, Present and Future." *Computers and Industrial Engineering* 43, no. 1, pp. 231–249.

Min, H., and S. Shin. 2012. "The Use of Radio Frequency Identification Technology for Managing the Global Supply Chain: An Exploratory Study of the Korean Logistics Industry." *International Journal of Logistics Systems and Management* 13, no. 3, pp. 269–286.

Min, S. 2001, "The Role of Marketing in Supply Chain Management," in *Supply Chain Management* edited by J.T. Mentzer, Thousand Oaks, CA: Sage Publications, Inc., 77–100.

Moore, L.G. April 30, 2012. "Matching Your Work to Patient Need." *Population Health*, http://www.treosolutions.com/blog/2012/04/matching-your-work-patient-need, (accessed February 1, 2014).

Munro, D. January 19, 2012. "U.S. Healthcare Hits $3 Trillion." *Forbes*, http://www.forbes.com/sites/danmunro/2012/01/19/u-s-healthcare-hits-3-trillion/, (accessed February 2, 2014).

NAPM InfoEdge. 2000. "Setting Up the Relationship to Succeed." *NAPM InfoEdge* 5, no. 2, pp. 13–15.

National Crime Prevention Council. 2014. *Counterfeit Drugs Are Bad Medicine*, http://www.ncpc.org/topics/intellectual-property-theft/counterfeit-drugs-1, (accessed February 14, 2014).

NEHI. 2014. *Waste and Inefficiency in Healthcare*, Unpublished Report, Cambridge, MA: New England Healthcare Institute, http://www.nehi.net/programs/17/waste_and_inefficiency_in_health_care

Nonaka, I. 1991. "The knowledge-creating company," *Harvard Business Review* 69, no. 6, pp. 96–104.

O'Connor, M.C. January 6, 2006. "Pfizer Using RFID to Fight Fake Viagra." *RFID Journal*, http://www.rfidjournal.com/articles/view?2075, (accessed February 14, 2014).

OECD. 2013. *Health at a Glance 2013: OECD Indicators*, Unpublished Report, Paris, France: OECD Publishing.

Office of the Inspector General. 2013. *Safe Harbor Regulations*. Washington, DC: U.S. Department of Health and Human Services, http://www.gpo.gov/fdsys/pkg/CFR-2010-title42-vol5/pdf/CFR-2010-title42-vol5-sec1001-952.pdf, (accessed January 23, 2014).

Oinas-Kukkonen, H., T. Räisänen, and N. Hummastenniemi. 2008. "Patient Relationship Management: An Overview and Study of a Follow-Up System." *Journal of Health Information Management* 28, no. 3, pp. 24–29.

Parvatiyar, A., and J.N. Sheth. 2001. "Conceptual Framework of Customer Relationship Management." In *Customer Relationship Management–Emerging Concepts, Tools, and Applications,* eds. J.N. Sheth, A. Parvatiyar, and G. Shainesh, 3–25. New York, NY: McGraw-Hill Education.

Perçin, S., and H. Min. 2013. "A Hybrid Quality Function Deployment and Fuzzy Multiple Objective Decision Making Approach to Selecting a Third-Party Logistics Service Provider." *International Journal of Logistics: Research and Applications* 16, no. 5, pp. 380–397.

Perera, G., A. Holbrook, L. Thabane, G. Foster, and D.J. Willison. 2011. "Views on Health Information Sharing and Privacy From Primary Care Practices Using Electronic Medical Records." *International Journal of Medical Informatics* 80, no. 2, pp. 94–101.

Pines, J.M., P.M. Mullins, J.K. Cooper, L.B. Feng, and K.E. Roth. 2013. "National Trends in Emergency Department Use, Care Patterns, and Quality of Care of Older Adults in the United States." *Journal of American Geriatric Society* 61, no. 1, pp. 12–17.

Poirier, C.C. 1999. *Advanced Supply Chain Management.* San Francisco, CA: Berrett-Koehler Publishers, Inc.

Porter, M.E. 1985. *Competitive Advantage: Creating and Sustaining Superior Performance.* New York, NY: The Free Press.

Practice Greenhealth. 2014. *Environmentally Preferable Purchasing,* https://practicegreenhealth.org/topics/epp, (accessed February 19, 2014).

Primary Healthcare, Inc. 2003. *Performance Improvement Plan,* Unpublished Report, Washington DC: Health Resources and Services Administration.

Pyzdek, T., and P.A. Keller. 2003. *The Six Sigma Handbook: A Complete Guide for Green belts, Black belts, and Managers at All Levels.* New York, NY: McGraw-Hill.

Ramsey, H. May 13, 2009. "Purdue Pharma Uses RFID to Combat Counterfeiting." *RFID Journal,* https://www.rfidjournal.com/purchase-access?type=Article&id=4889&r=%2Farticles%2Fview%3F4889, (accessed February 14, 2014).

Reay, P., A. Casebeer, K. Golden-Biddle, and C.R. Hinings. 2009. *Organizational Learning in Primary Healthcare Innovation,* Unpublished Report, FRN #78710, Edmonton, Canada: The Canadian Institutes of Health Research (CIHR).

Reinhardt, U.E. 2006. "The Pricing of US Hospital Services: Chaos Behind a Veil of Secrecy." *Health Affairs* 25, no. 1, pp. 57–69.

Report of the International Federation of Pharmaceutical Manufacturers and Associations. 2013. *Facts and Figures 2012.* Geneva, Switzerland: IFPMA.

ReVelle, C. 1989. "Review, Extension, and Prediction in Emergency Service Siting Models." *European Journal of Operational Research* 40, no. 1, pp. 58–69.

Robbins, G., A. Robbins, and J.C. Goodman. 1994. *Inefficiency in the US Healthcare System: What Can We Do?*, NCPA Policy Report No. 182, Dallas, TX: National Center for Policy Analysis.

Rosenbaum, S. 2011. "The Patient Protection and Affordable Care Act: Implications for Public Health Policy and Practice." *Public Health Reports* 126, no. 1, p. 130.

Rother, M., and J. Shook. 2003. *Learning to See: Value-Stream Mapping to Create Value and Eliminate Muda: Version 1.3.* Brookline, MA: Lean Enterprise Institute.

Sanders, N.R. 2012. *Supply Chain Management: A Global Perspective.* Hoboken, NJ: John Wiley & Sons.

Schotanus, F., and J. Telgen. 2007. "Developing a Typology of Organizational Forms of Cooperative Purchasing." *Journal of Purchasing and Supply Management* 13, no. 1, pp. 53–68.

Schultz, G.P. 1970. "The Logic of Healthcare Facility Planning." *Socio-Economic Planning Sciences* 4, no. 3, pp. 383–393.

Shank, J.K., and V. Govindarajan. 1993. *Strategic Cost Management: The New Tool for Competitive Advantage.* New York, NY: The Free Press.

Simcich, T. 2014. "Buy Green, Save Green." *Green Purchasing*, Department of Ecology in the State of Washington, http://www.ecy.wa.gov/programs/swfa/epp/, (accessed February 19, 2014).

Sink, H.L., and C.J. Langley. 1997. "A Managerial Framework for the Acquisition of Third-Party Logistics Services." *Journal of Business Logistics* 18, no. 2, pp. 163–187.

Sinkula, J.M. 1994. "Market Information Processing and Organizational Learning." *Journal of Marketing* 58, no. 1, pp. 35–45.

Smolka, G., M. Multack, and C. Figueiredo. 2012. *Health Insurance Coverage for 50- to 64-Year-Olds*, Unpublished Report, Issue 59, Washington, DC: AARP Public Policy Institute.

Snow, S. 2013. *Medical Tourism Around the World*, Unpublished Report, http://visual.ly/medical-tourism-around-world?utm_source=visually_embed, (accessed February 22, 2014).

Social Security Administration. 2013. *Annual Statistical Report on the Social Security Disability Insurance Program 2012*, SSA Publication No. 13-11826, Washington, DC: Social Security Administration.

Students for Sustainability. 2014. "What Is Sustainability and Why Is It So Important?" Ottawa, Ontario, Canada: Canadian Federation of Students and The David Suzuki Foundation. http://studentsforsustainability.ca/index.php?section_id=53

Svoboda, S. 1995. *Note on Life Cycle Analysis*, Unpublished Report, National Pollution Prevention Center, Ann Arbor, MI: University of Michigan.

Tansel, B.C., R.L. Francis, and T.J. Lowe. 1983. "State of the Art—Location on Networks: A Survey. Part I: The p-center and p-median Problems." *Management Science* 29, no. 4, pp. 482–497.

Teichgräber, U.K., and M. de Bucourt. 2012. "Applying Value Stream Mapping Techniques to Eliminate Non-Value-Added Waste for the Procurement of Endovascular Stents." *European Journal of Radiology* 81, no. 1, pp. e47–e52.

ten Ham, M. 2003. "Health Risks of Counterfeit Pharmaceuticals." *Drug Safety* 26, no. 14, pp. 991–997.

The Associated Press. November 23, 2013. "Victims of Compounding Pharmacy's Tainted Steroids Face Mounting Frustration." *CBS Boston*, http://boston.cbslocal.com/2013/11/24/victims-of-compounding-pharmacys-tainted-steroids-face-mounting-frustration/, (accessed February 12, 2014).

The Association of the Automatic Identification and Data Capture Industry. 2002. *Radio Frequency Identification: A Basic Primer*, White Paper, Pittsburgh, PA, http://www.aimglobal.org.

The Association of the British Pharmaceutical Industry. 2012. *Global Pharmaceutical Industry and Market*, http://www.abpi.org.uk/industry-info/knowledge-hub/global-industry/Pages/industry-market-.aspx#fig1, (accessed February 17, 2014).

Thomas G., Reddy, S., and Oliel, S. 2014. "Global health workforce shortage to reach 12.9 million in coming decades," *World Health Organization*, http://www.who.int/mediacentre/news/releases/2013/health-workforce-shortage/en/, retrieved on March 12, 2014.

Topol, E.J. 2004. "Intensive Statin Therapy-A Sea Change in Cardiovascular Prevention." *New England Journal of Medicine* 350, no. 15, pp. 1562–1564.

Transparency Market Research. 2013. *Medical Tourism Market - Global Industry Analysis, Size, Share, Growth, Trends and Forecast, 2013–2019*, Unpublished Report, Albany, New York: Transparency Market Research.

U.S. Census Bureau. 2013. "2012 National Population Projections: Summary Tables." Washington, DC: U.S. Census Bureau, http://www.census.gov/population/age/

U.S. Department of Health and Human Services. June 28, 2012. *Affordable Care Act*, http://www.hhs.gov/healthcare/rights/law/, (accessed January 30, 2014).

U.S. Food and Drug Administration. 2005. "RFID: Protecting the Drug Supply." *FDA Consumer Magazine*, http://www.fda.gov/Drugs/DrugSafety/ucm169918.htm, (accessed February, 14, 2014).

van der Meer, W., and J. Kerkhofs. 2008. *The Art of Pricing in the Pharmaceutical Industry*, Unpublished White Paper, Zurich, Switzerland: Lodestone Management Consultants.

Visiongain. 2014. *The 3D Printing Market for Healthcare Will Reach $4043m in 2018*, https://www.visiongain.com/Press_Release/553/The-3D-Printing-market-for-Healthcare-will-reach-4043m-in-2018-predicts-new-study, (accessed February 26, 2014).

Walker, H., F. Schotanus, E. Bakker, and C. Harland. 2013. "Collaborative Procurement: A Relational View of Buyer–Buyer Relationships." *Public Administration Review* 73, no. 4, pp. 588–598.

Walker, J., E. Pan, D. Johnston, J. Adler-Milstein, D.W. Bates, and B. Middleton. January 19, 2005. "The Value of Healthcare Information Exchange and Interoperability." *Health Affairs-Health Track Market Watch*, January 19, http://content.healthaffairs.org/content/suppl/2005/02/07/hlthaff.w5.10.DC1, retrieved on March 15, 2014.

Waters, W. 2014. *EPP Case Study: Compostable Coolers at Fairview Health Services*, Unpublished Report, Reston, VA: A Practice Greenhealth Initiative.

WebMD. October 27, 2011. "What are Outpatient Services." *WebMD Medical Reference from Healthwise*, http://www.webmd.com/a-to-z-guides/outpatient-services-learning-about-outpatient-services, (accessed February 7, 2014).

Weintraub, K. March 20, 2014. "Millions More Could Get Statin Drugs." *USA Today*, p. 3A.

World Bank. 2013. *World Development Indicators: Health Systems*, http://data.worldbank.org/indicator/SH.XPD.TOTL.ZS, (accessed January 22, 2014).

World Health Organization. 2008. *Integrated Health Services – What and Why?*, Unpublished Report, Technical Brief No. 1, Geneva, Switzerland: WHO.

World Health Organization. 2011. *Waste from Health-care Activities*, http://www.who.int/mediacentre/factsheets/fs253/en/, (accessed February 18, 2014).

World Health Organization. 2014a. *Pharmaceutical Industry*, http://www.who.int/trade/glossary/story073/en/, (accessed February 9, 2014).

World Health Organization. 2014b. *What are Counterfeit Medicines?*, http://www.who.int/medicines/services/counterfeit/faqs/03/en/, (accessed February 12, 2014).

Yao, W., C.H. Chu, and Z. Li. 2012. "The Adoption and Implementation of RFID Technologies in Healthcare: A Literature Review." *Journal of Medical Systems* 36, no. 6, pp. 3507–3525.

Zhou, G., H. Min, C. Xu, and Z. Cao. 2008. "Evaluating the Comparative Efficiency of Chinese Third-Party Logistics Providers Using Data Envelopment Analysis." *International Journal of Physical Distribution and Logistics Management* 38, no. 4, pp. 262–279.

Index

OTHER FORTHCOMING TITLES FROM THE HEALTHCARE MANAGEMENT COLLECTION

David Dilts, Oregon Health & Science University (OHSU)
and Lawrence Fredendall, Clemson University, Editors

- *Quality Management in a Lean Health Care Environment* by Melissa Mannon, and Daniel Collins
- *Achieving Patient and Caregiver Satisfaction in Health Care: How the HCAHPS Findings Can Help Foster Positive Perceptions that Lead to Increased Revenues* by James Driscoll
- *Management Skills for Clinicians: Making the Transition from Patient Care to Health Care Administration* by Linda LaGanga

Business Expert Press has over 30 collection in business subjects such as finance, marketing strategy, sustainability, public relations, economics, accounting, corporate communications, and many others. For more information about all our collections, please visit www. businessexpertpress.com/collections.

Announcing the Business Expert Press Digital Library

*Concise E-books Business Students Need
for Classroom and Research*

This book can also be purchased in an e-book collection by your library as
- a one-time purchase,
- that is owned forever,
- allows for simultaneous readers,
- has no restrictions on printing, and
- can be downloaded as PDFs from within the library community.

Our digital library collections are a great solution to beat the rising cost of textbooks. E-books can be loaded into their course management systems or onto students' e-book readers.

The **Business Expert Press** digital libraries are very affordable, with no obligation to buy in future years. For more information, please visit **www.businessexpertpress.com/librarians**. To set up a trial in the United States, please email **sales@businessexpertpress.com**.

CPSIA information can be obtained
at www.ICGtesting.com
Printed in the USA
BVHW092332250621
610172BV00007BA/119

9 781606 498941